Katherine Muncaster
with Shirley Clarke

Growth Mindset Lessons

Every child a learner

Dedication

This book is dedicated to my wonderful daughter Emily who inspires me, makes me smile and encourages me to use my own growth mindset.

Katherine Muncaster

I would like to thank Katherine Muncaster for developing these wonderful lessons. Through her determination to give every child in her school a growth mindset, she will have changed the lives of so many, more profoundly than she probably realises or would take credit for. You are an inspiration to me, Katherine.

Shirley Clarke

Every effort has been made to trace all copyright holders, but if any have been inadvertently overlooked, the Publishers will be pleased to make the necessary arrangements at the first opportunity.

This title contains links to videos on YouTube and other websites not owned or controlled by Rising Stars. Every effort has been made to ensure that these videos do not infringe copyright. If any copyright infringement has been overlooked, the publisher will be pleased to make the necessary arrangements at the next opportunity.

Although every effort has been made to ensure that website addresses are correct at time of going to press, Rising Stars cannot be held responsible for the content of any website mentioned in this book. It is sometimes possible to find a relocated web page by typing in the address of the home page for a website in the URL window of your browser.

Hachette UK's policy is to use papers that are natural, renewable and recyclable products and made from wood grown in sustainable forests. The logging and manufacturing processes are expected to conform to the environmental regulations of the country of origin.

Orders: please contact Bookpoint Ltd, 130 Park Drive, Milton Park, Abingdon, Oxon OX14 4SE. Telephone: (44) 01235 827720. Fax: (44) 01235 400454. Email education@bookpoint.co.uk. Lines are open from 9 a.m. to 5 p.m., Monday to Saturday, with a 24-hour message answering service.

ISBN: 978 1 4718 9368 1

© Katherine Muncaster and Shirley Clarke 2016

First published in 2016 by

Rising Stars UK Ltd, part of Hodder Education Group
An Hachette UK Company
Carmelite House
50 Victoria Embankment
London EC4Y 0DZ

www.risingstars-uk.com

Impression number 10 9 8 7 6 5 4 3 2 1

Year   2020 2019 2018 2017 2016

Cover photo © Anita Ponne//Shutterstock.com

Illustrations by Aptara, Inc.

Typeset in India

Printed in Italy

A catalogue record for this title is available from the British Library.

The Publishers would like to thank the following for permission to reproduce copyright material.

Photo credits

If a photo is not credited here, it is © Katherine Muncaster 2016.

p17 © EvgenySHCH – Shutterstock **p73** © Jack.Q – Fotolia; © Hans-Peter Moehlig / Fotolia **p85** © Kokoulina – Shutterstock **p99** © Vixit – Shutterstock **p115** © Kaliva – Shutterstock **p117** © Kaliva – Shutterstock **p123** © Ksenia Raykova – Shutterstock; © Robyn Mackenzie – Shutterstock; © fotograzia / iStockphoto; © andreistanciulescu – Fotolia; © Steve Cukrov – Shutterstock; **p124** © Rita Kochmarjova – Shutterstock **p133 (from left to right)** © Michael Steele/Getty Images, © AF archive / Alamy Stock Photo, © WENN Ltd / Alamy Stock Photo, © Paolo Bona - Shutterstock **p136** © Leah-Anne Thompson – Shutterstock **p149** © STILLFX –Shutterstock; © Comstock Images/Getty Images / Sports Icons KCD092 **p157** © Artem Kovalenco – Shutterstock; © Sebastian Kaulitzki – Shutterstock; © HitToon – Shutterstock; © 997 C Squared Studios/ Photodisc / Getty Images / Eat, Drink, Dine 48; © Kaissa – Shutterstock **p170** © emanelda – Fotolia; © Peter Titmuss – Shutterstock; © KK Art and Photography – Shutterstock **p185** © urfin – Shutterstock; © Creative Crop/Digital Vision/Getty Images; © Steve Cole/Photodisc/Getty Images / Festivities OS19 **p201** © Tony Gable and C Squared Studios/Photodisc/Getty Images/ Musical Instruments 34; © Sebastian Kaulitzki – Shutterstock **p220** © Juan Gaertner – Shutterstock; © kosmos111 – Shutterstock; © Aleksey Stemmer -Shutterstock; © Ulf Thurmann – Shutterstock

Acknowledgements

p5 Copyright © Mindset Works, Inc. All rights reserved. Used with permission. Additional resources at www. mindsetworks.com **p6** © Adapted from Education Week *"Carol Dweck Revisits the 'Growth Mindset' "* Sept 23, 2015. Reprinted with permission from the author **p14** © Carol Dweck and adapted from mindsetonline.com, 2006 (permission sought) **p190, p191 and p192** The Iceberg Illusion © Sylvia Duckworth **p210** © MakeBeliefsComix

Acknowledgements

This book has been a labour of love and it would not have been possible without Shirley Clarke. Thank you for encouraging me to write this book, for your feedback, advice and inspirational work. Thanks also to Katie Blainey at Rising Stars for being excited at the prospect of this book!

Thank you to all of the wonderful teachers, teaching assistants, parents and children at Ludworth Primary School who have supported, encouraged and provided such useful feedback: Jenny Cartwright, Kath Donoghue, Frank Earp, Gaynor Kelly, Candice Kossowska, Rachel MacKinnon, Becci Naughton, Emily Pond, Denise Storey and Natalie Welsh.

Also the talented teaching assistants who have helped bring my display ideas to life: Denise Ambrey, Cath Hargreaves, Heather Hoyle, Clare Spink and Lynne Taylor.

Special thanks to Martin Stamper for the amazing photographs that I have used to document my mindset journey, Joan Walker for her wonderful artwork and drawings of the brain and Sylvia Duckworth for the introduction to sketchnoting and her amazing creations.

Thank you to Roary Pownall – it was a privilege to work for you and I learnt so much.

A huge thank you to Moira Rayner for her support, words of wisdom and encouragement and many thanks to the Marple Learning Team, especially Maria Walters for her advice, support and cake!

Finally, my love and thanks to my amazing family – my mum, dad and siblings David and Suzie, all of whom have always encouraged me to work hard and believe in myself.

Katherine Muncaster

Downloadable resources

There are free video clips and other useful resources related to this book on the Rising Stars website. Look out for the square QR codes throughout the book, as well as the accompanying links.

To access the downloadable resources via the QR codes, you will need a QR code reader for your smartphone/tablet. There are many free readers available, depending on the smartphone/tablet you are using.

Once you have downloaded a QR code reader, simply open the reader app and use it to take a photo of the code. The page will then load on your smartphone/tablet.

If you cannot read the QR code or you are using a computer, the web link next to the code will take you to the same place.

The link below will allow you to access a master page with links to all the downloadable resources for this book. You can also use the QR code on the right to access the same page.

bit.ly/2esr2M0

Contents

Introduction by Shirley Clarke   1

Introduction by Katherine Muncaster   7

How to use this book   15

Three assemblies   25

    1   *Zootropolis* … rising to new challenges   25

    2   Learning from our mistakes   27

    3   *The Dot* (from small beginnings …)   30

Lessons for 4–5 year olds (Reception, UK)   33

1   'Help! I'm stuck!'   35

2   Everyone can learn to ride a bicycle   38

3   Incy Wincy Spider   41

4   Cleversticks   44

5   Toppling towers   48

6   Rooting for you   52

Lessons for 5–6 year olds (Year 1, UK)   55

1   I give up!   56

2   Strictly can't dance   59

3   Grow, grow, grow your brain   63

4   Soaking up the learning   69

5   Super snails 1 – the power of perseverance   72

6   Super snails 2 – setting challenges   75

Lessons for 6–7 year olds (Year 2, UK)   79

1   Playing teacher   81

2   'Oh no! I've made a mistake!'   84

3   'Girls can't do that!' Dream big!   88

4   Super effort   91

5   Challenge mountains   99

6   Ding ding! How much effort?   103

Lessons for 7–8 year olds (Year 3, UK)   107

1   On the high wire   108
2   Firing neurons   111
3   Born to be …   114
4   Mistakes that worked   122
5   Challenge mountains   127
6   Never give up!   129

Lessons for 8–9 year olds (Year 4, UK)   131

1   From failure to success   132
2   Bounce!   136
3   Doom words   141
4   Mindset trumps   144
5   Fantastic elastic brain   149
6   Learning cereals   155

Lessons for 9–10 year olds (Year 5, UK)   159

1   Passport to learning   160
2   Too old to …   166
3   What makes a great teacher?   169
4   Brain power!   179
5   Famous failures   184
6   The iceberg illusion   189

Lessons for 10–11 year olds (Year 6, UK)   195

1   'Don't say … Say …'   196
2   Diamond minds   201
3   Barriers to learning   207
4   Brain v calculator   211
5   Mathematical mistakes   215
6   Learning pathways   219

References and resources   223

Introduction by Shirley Clarke

The term 'growth mindset' was coined by Professor Carol Dweck at Stanford University as a result of her quest spanning more than 30 years to find out what motivates us to learn. She synthesised all the studies to do with motivation, including many of her own, and gave us a deceptively simple but accessible way of understanding what matters: the fixed and growth mindsets.

Brain truths and myths

First, let's look at what we know about the brain, as this is central to the notion of mindsets. People with a fixed mindset believe they are born with a certain amount of intelligence and that is that for the rest of their lives. People with a growth mindset, however, know that intelligence is not fixed and that you can, in effect, 'grow' your intelligence. Brain research has confirmed this.

We now know that the brain can be developed like a muscle, changing and growing stronger the more it is used. The brain grows new cells when we are learning new information and skills. Older people can also develop their brains in an enriched environment.

Carol Dweck, in her online article entitled 'You can grow your intelligence' (2011), explains in simple terms how the brain works. Many teachers use this article to introduce the workings of the brain to their pupils.

> 'Inside the cortex of the brain are billions of tiny nerve cells, called neurons. The nerve cells have branches connecting them to other cells in a complicated network. Communication between these brain cells is what allows us to think and solve problems.
>
> When you learn new things, these tiny connections in the brain actually multiply and get stronger. The more that you challenge your mind to learn, the more your brain cells grow. Then, things that you once found very hard or even impossible to do – like speaking a foreign language or doing algebra – seem to become easy. The result is a stronger, smarter brain.'

Dweck (2011)

Research into the brains of London taxi drivers (Woollett and Maguire, 2012) discovered that the huge amount of memory they had to use to learn 'The Knowledge' – that is, every street in inner and outer London – resulted in a slightly enlarged area of the hippocampus. These drivers could also memorise other things easily as a result of this effect. Similarly, people who have, for many years, learnt a musical instrument which uses fingering, find it easy to learn to type, because the connections made in the brain for the instrument are the same as those needed for typing. Once the neural connections have been made repeatedly, the pathways become more fixed.

Making children aware of these facts and, for example, showing them YouTube clips of neurons connecting, leads to children being able to identify when they can feel their brain 'growing'. 'This is really making me think! I can feel my neurons connecting!' is a commonly heard cry in such a learning culture.

People used to think that intelligence tests conferred a lifelong score, but we now know this is incorrect. The score is simply an indicator of the person's achievement at that time and not a predictor of future achievement. This is the same with any test, unless there are severe learning impairments. I urge teachers to use the terms 'lower achievers' and 'higher achievers' because these imply performance 'at this moment' as opposed to 'high ability' and 'low ability' or 'able' and 'less able' which imply permanence.

The route to developing a 'smarter' brain is input, practice and effort. We all come to school at different stages in our development for certain subjects or skills based on how or whether our genes have been expressed, together with the influence of our home environment. This is one reason why, at an early age, so many of us write off certain subjects when we compare ourselves to others who are seemingly more adept. It is important to know that, with varying amounts of **time**, **effort**, **practice** and **input**, we could all reach a required level of proficiency. A crucial component of the learning culture in the classroom is to continually talk with pupils about how the brain grows, how we can grow our abilities by practising and through input, and the gift of being able to learn from one another and so tapping all our different strengths.

Fixed mindsets and growth mindsets

The notion of a growth mindset (Dweck, 2000) has become an accessible concept to describe the way learners need to feel about themselves and their abilities in order to be successful learners. Research over many years has highlighted that we all differ as learners, being mostly fixed or mostly growth, and differing in different situations. Figure 1 highlights the differences between the two mindsets.

Fixed mindset (performance orientation)	Growth mindset (learning orientation)
Intelligence is static. **I must look clever!**	**Intelligence is expandable.** **I want to learn more!**
Avoids challenges	Embraces challenges
Gives up easily	Persists in the face of setbacks
Sees effort as pointless	Sees effort as the way
Ignores useful criticism	Learns from criticism
⬇	⬇
Likely to plateau early and achieve less than full potential	*Reaches ever higher levels of achievement*

Figure 1 Fixed versus growth mindsets

A fixed mindset is the result of a continual focus on your ability rather than on your achievement and effort. Praise to infants onwards reinforcing 'cleverness' or intelligence and exclaiming about the speed of mastery gives children a clear subliminal message: to get approval you need to master new things quickly and with little effort, both of which will earn you the 'clever' label. The more your ability, your speed and lack of effort is praised ('Well done! You hardly needed to think about/work at that at all!' or 'Clever girl!'), the more you will not want to lose that position of greatness, so the less you want to engage in tasks which require time or effort or might lead to some kind of failure. People with a fixed mindset avoid challenging tasks for fear of failure, thus missing many valuable learning opportunities.

Many studies (for example, Black and Wiliam, 1998; Butler, 1988; Cameron and Pierce, 1994), show that rewards (that is, a concrete version of grades given to a select few for their achievement, effort or behaviour) reinforce a fixed mindset, both for those who get the reward and those who do not. Children do not need rewards when the culture is focused around all children competing against themselves and their own previous achievement. When there is a growth mindset culture in which the learner's achievement is celebrated verbally and personally and the goal is to strive for excellence, stickers and stars are tokenistic and patronising.

The following table (Figure 2) was included in 'Mindsetworks' (mindsetworks.com), an invaluable online resource linked with Carol Dweck's research. It shows how the different mindsets affect the effort a learner applies to a task. We are all somewhere on the continuum between having a fixed mindset or a growth mindset, so the addition of the 'mixed' column helps to identify some of the features and therefore needs of those children in-between the two mindsets. This might be especially useful when establishing a rough baseline of children's current mindsets.

	Fixed	Mixed	Growth
Taking on challenges	You don't really take on challenges on your own. You feel that challenges are to be avoided.	You might take on challenges when you have some previous experience with success in a related challenge.	You look forward to the next challenge and have long range plans for new challenges.
Learning from mistakes	You see mistakes as failures, as proof that the task is beyond your reach. You may hide mistakes or lie about them.	You may accept mistakes as temporary setbacks, but lack strategies to apply what you learned from the mistakes in order to succeed.	You see mistakes as temporary setbacks, something to be overcome. You reflect about what you learned and apply that learning when revisiting the task.

Accepting feedback and criticism	You feel threatened by feedback and may avoid it altogether. Criticism and constructive feedback are seen as a reason to quit.	You may be motivated by feedback if it is not overly critical or threatening. Who is giving the feedback, the level of difficulty of the task, or their personal feelings might all be factors in your motivation.	You invite and are motivated by feedback and criticism. You apply new strategies as a result of feedback. You think of feedback as being a supportive element in the learning process.
Practise and applying strategies	You do not practise and avoid practising when you can. You do not have any strategies for accomplishing the learning goals or tasks, or you apply ineffective strategies.	You practise, but a big setback can make you want to quit. You are more willing to practise things you are already considered good at. You are open to being given a strategy to meet a challenge, but you rarely apply your own strategies unless it is something you are already good at.	You enjoy the process of practising and see it as part of the process of getting good at something. You may create your own practice or study plans. You fluidly use many strategies, think of some of your own strategies and ask others about their strategies.
Perseverance and focus	You have little persistence on learning goals and tasks. You give up at the first sign of a struggle.	You may persevere with prompting and support. Unless you are provided with strategies for overcoming obstacles, you will stop or give up.	You 'stick to it' and have stamina for the task(s). You keep working confidently until the task is complete.

Asking questions	You do not ask questions or do not know which questions to ask, but you can usually say you 'don't get it' if asked.	You might ask questions about a portion of the task that you feel you can do. If you perceive it to be out of your ability, you probably won't ask questions.	You ask specific questions, ask questions about your own thinking and challenge the text, the task and the teacher.
Taking risks	You do not take risks, and if something is too hard you give in blank or copied work, if anything at all. You are not engaged in the process/task.	You will take risks if the task is already fairly familiar to you. If not, you will resort to copying or giving in partially completed work.	You begin tasks confidently, risk making errors and openly share the work you produce.

Figure 2 How mindset affects effort, Mindset Works Inc (mindsetworks.com), 2012

Carol Dweck's latest thoughts about the mindsets

In late 2015, Dweck wrote an article airing some of her observations and concerns about the implementation of the growth mindset. She wrote:

1 A growth mindset isn't just about effort. Students need to try new strategies and seek input from others when they're stuck – a repertoire of strategies.

2 Don't praise effort if no learning has happened. Say 'Let's talk about what you've tried and what you can try next.'

3 The growth mindset was intended to close achievement gaps, not hide them, so don't tell them everyone is smart or that just putting in effort is enough.

4 Don't use the fixed mindset to blame children – 'Oh, he has a fixed mindset' – rather than your teaching.

5 Don't just talk about the growth mindset – your words and actions must follow. If you react to mistakes as though they are problems rather than helpful, students will develop fixed mindsets.

6 Acknowledge fixed mindset feelings and work with and through them.

'Mindsets revisited', *Education Week*, September 23, 2015. Published online.

Finally, we need to find the right words when children tell us they are stuck or do not understand something so that we create a culture where mistakes and lack of understanding are normalised: they are an opportunity for new learning to take place and vital feedback for the teacher. Dweck suggests words to use and words not to use (see Figure 3).

What not to say (fixed mindset)	What to say (growth mindset)
Not everybody is good at maths. Just do your best.	When you learn how to do a new kind of problem, it grows your maths brain!
That's OK. Maybe maths isn't one of your strengths.	If you catch yourself saying 'I'm no good at maths', just add the word 'yet' to the end of the sentence.
Don't worry. You'll get it if you keep trying. (If students are using the wrong strategies, their efforts might not work. They may also feel particularly inept if their efforts are fruitless.)	That feeling of maths being hard is the feeling of your brain growing.
Great effort! You tried your best. (Don't accept less than optimal performance from your students.)	The point isn't to get it all right away. The point is to grow your understanding step by step. What can you try next?

Figure 3 What to say and what *not to say*

'*Mindsets revisited*', *Education* Week, Carol Dweck, September 2015.

Bringing the growth mindset to life

This book is the result of Katherine's passionate vision to make the growth mindset a living, breathing culture throughout Ludworth School. The lessons and activities embody the spirit and the precision of Carol Dweck's growth mindset, thus enabling all teachers to more easily follow their example and help create highly confident, error-enjoying, risk-taking learners.

Introduction by Katherine Muncaster

Children need to be prepared for an ever-changing world. The teaching of mindsets builds resilience and a desire to learn, to challenge themselves and to encourage others – all of which are necessary for children's future success.

This book takes the abstract concept of mindsets and turns it into a series of engaging lessons for every year of the primary school. It provides practical classroom activities and strategies to foster the development of a growth mindset and an effective learning culture. The teaching of growth mindsets has had a huge impact in my school: it has raised standards, built resilience and created a culture of collaborative learning in both the classroom and the staffroom. With Shirley Clarke's encouragement and support, I have written this book to share our journey with you.

Developing growth mindsets in Ludworth School

My mindset journey began over seven years ago, after being inspired while listening to Shirley Clarke describe Carol Dweck's concept of the growth mindset. I was eager to develop this with younger children and to turn an abstract concept into something practical and engaging. I wanted to provide children with the opportunity to discuss and reflect on learning and their own learning journey.

I am passionate about learning and not placing limits on children's learning journeys. Dweck's work clearly demonstrates the impact mindset has on children and their learning: embracing a growth mindset enables children to aspire and achieve their true potential.

In order for children to develop their awareness of mindsets and change their own learning behaviour, I believe it is essential that the concept of mindsets is explicitly taught and explored by children.

Embedding the mindsets

My aim has been to develop a whole-school approach to mindsets with structured, meaningful activities that provide children with the opportunity to discuss, reflect and respond to learning. The lessons support schools in providing a consistent approach to mindsets and, over time, can help the concept and culture of mindsets to become embedded across the whole school.

My objective was to ensure that mindsets run through every aspect of school like the lettering on a stick of rock. This takes considerable time and it was vital to have all staff on board, embracing the idea and valuing its impact.

Stage 1: Pilot with Year 2

Initially, I piloted my ideas for the teaching of the growth mindset with the 6 and 7 year olds in Year 2. As I was their class teacher, this allowed me to experiment with my practice. In addition, there is national data for Year 2 which allowed me to analyse the impact of the work. I was fortunate to work in a two-form entry school, with a highly experienced colleague who was willing to come on the journey with me. The pilot consisted of a series of lessons that explored the concept of the growth mindset.

Introducing the concept

Initially I wrote a simple story set in a school where children demonstrated the different mindset behaviours and shared this with the children. This introduced the concept and allowed the children to discuss the different learning behaviours.

Reinforcing the concept

Follow-up lessons introduced the idea of working in a learning group and included a discussion on how to support a child with a fixed mindset. Other lessons included a debate about whether you were born to be in a particular job and setting personal challenges to improve your learning behaviour. Throughout these lessons, and at every meaningful opportunity, we reinforced the concept of the growth mindset and its different characteristics.

Reviewing teacher feedback

We also reviewed our classroom practice, focusing on feedback. Initially, we felt that the culture of our classrooms encouraged children to make mistakes and that it supported children as incremental learners, yet we were finding that we had a growing number of children who would be classed as having a fixed mindset. It was becoming increasingly common, for instance, for our 'gifted and talented' children to exhibit the attributes of a fixed mindset in areas that they found more challenging.

Developing the feedback and normalising mistakes

In the classroom, we developed the feedback that we used and began to identify challenges for the children (the next step in their learning). This was then developed further by the children identifying their own challenges. Some children also identified challenges for their peers. We began to openly discuss mistakes that we had made and then developed this further by identifying mistakes that children had made. We encouraged the children to see mistakes as a key part of the learning process.

The word began to spread ...

Piloting mindsets in only one year group slowly created a buzz around the school. Both staff and children began to ask questions about mindsets and were eager to learn more. Often siblings of children in Year 2 would learn about mindsets at home as the children shared their journey and explained the concept. Piloting in a key area of the school helped mindsets develop momentum and captured people's interest.

Refining the learning through action research

As part of the initial pilot in Year 2, I received funding for a small scale research project that examined the impact of teaching the concept of growth mindsets to children who had been identified as gifted and talented. The study lasted six months and focused on six children, looking at their academic progress and attitudes to learning. The children all had the same experiences as their peers – the direct teaching, changes to feedback and the sharing of mistakes as part of the learning process. The key difference was that we recorded and reflected on their learning behaviours in greater detail.

The process of action research was instrumental in refining my work. It also raised the profile of pupil voice as the pupils were interviewed regularly and the culture in the classroom changed as children were given more opportunities for focused meaningful talk. I would highly recommend action research or lesson study as a means of improving both your own practice and your practice in school.

Impact: in school

It became apparent that all the Year 2 pupils' mindsets changed considerably through this process. We gathered evidence for this from lesson observations, from teacher and parent feedback, from the children's responses to our questionnaires and from observing their attitudes in class.

They became much more aware of the way they approached learning and how to be more effective. Their behaviour and attitudes to work altered and this was displayed in areas that previously they had found difficult or in which they had appeared complacent. It is particularly interesting to note that the areas in which the children made most progress were areas where class teachers felt they were under-performing. Boys were more often engaged in writing and girls became more confident to have a go in maths.

Most of the children developed a desire for a challenge and two of the six focus children appeared to no longer be motivated by extrinsic rewards: instead they were motivated by their own satisfaction. A key element in my approach was the involvement of the children in this process. I endeavoured to respond to their ideas in lessons, such as acting on their suggestions for further debates for future lessons. Often their ideas enhanced and stimulated the learning further.

I also sought feedback on my teaching and how it helped them to learn and if there were any aspects I could do differently. Providing the children with the opportunity to share feedback on my teaching helped to develop the classroom culture of everyone as a learner. The children become more open and responsive to feedback to each other and themselves. Identifying their own targets, and breaking them down into manageable steps, engaged them in their own learning. One girl, age 7, during the pilot in 2010 described her learning journey:

> ❛I am going to develop my brain by thinking it is OK to make mistakes. You need to not cry but think of the work that you have done when you were younger and see what progress you have made.❜

Impact: outside school

The children involved in this study were only 6–7 years old, yet they were able to internalise the concept of growth mindsets. Their parents commented on the children's discussions at home about the concepts and how they were also using their growth mindsets outside school. The transference of growth mindsets from being a concept taught at school to one the children were using in everyday life is an indicator of the extent to which the children had embraced the idea. It also demonstrates the potential the teaching of the concept has, particularly if there is greater parental involvement.

During the pilot, parents provided a considerable amount of helpful anecdotal evidence of the impact of mindsets and the changes to their children's learning behaviours. The children were the key to engaging parents with the concept as they went home, sharing ideas with their parents and persuading them to use their own growth mindset. We then developed this further by asking for feedback through a parental questionnaire and inviting parents to presentations on how the school was developing its approach to mindsets. We shared video clips of children discussing how learning about mindsets had changed them as learners and the impact it had on them. This proved to be an extremely powerful tool.

Stage 2: Whole-school involvement

Initial staff meetings

The following year, my Year 2 colleague and I introduced the concept to the whole school in a staff meeting. The pilot enabled us to learn from our mistakes and create resources to use in staff meetings such as video clips.

The staff meeting began by staff independently completing and then scoring Dweck's questionnaire 'Implicit Theories of Intelligence Scale for Children'. This is found at the end of her book *Self-theories: their role in motivation, personality and development* (2000). The concept of growth and fixed mindsets was then introduced and the key features shared. The presentation was interspersed with video clips of our children discussing the effect mindsets had had on their learning. Following the staff meeting, the teachers then used Dweck's questionnaire with older children and a modified version with younger children (see Figure 4 at the end of this section).

A follow-up staff meeting focused on introducing the initial lessons I had designed to introduce the concept across school, and we watched clips of lessons from Year 2. We emphasised developing the teacher's role as a facilitator in learning. Initially this was quite challenging for some staff, as stepping back and having a less active role in the lessons was a new experience and it took time to develop the different skills needed as a facilitator.

Staff support

Team teaching

Time was set aside for me to work alongside class teachers to team-teach and to support the implementation. Spending time with colleagues teaching together, discussing learning and observing children was invaluable. This led to a deeper level of discussion about learning between staff.

Staff performance management objectives were linked to work on the implementation of the growth mindset while lesson observations focused on how the children discussed their learning and how teachers gave feedback, all of which reinforced the concept.

Teaching assistants

Teaching assistants also received training about growth mindsets, focusing on how to give effective feedback and how to nurture and challenge children's learning. The training session began with an introduction to the two different mindsets and staff had the opportunity to discuss children's behaviour that reflected these. I explored the impact that the different mindsets had on children as learners and how the feedback we give children affects this. The session concluded with staff developing different approaches to feedback, including the idea of challenging children by giving specific feedback on how they could improve.

Parents

I also ran another information evening for parents, at which I explained the concepts and how they could support their child at home. The meeting for parents involved a brief introduction to the concept of mindsets and the research and why it was important. I then shared the school's new approaches to feedback and used video clips of children talking about the positive impact that mindsets had on them as a learner. I then outlined the key principles behind our teaching of mindsets and examples of the lessons and activities that the children would be exploring. Finally, I explained some practical strategies that parents could use to support their child in understanding the concept of mindsets.

Evidence collection

At the end of the year, children were asked to complete the mindset questionnaire again and children from every year group were filmed being interviewed. I also used a group of Year 6 children (10–11 year olds) to interview others to enable the children to answer questions more openly. The children's responses had altered significantly and the children were now identifying themselves and their learning behaviour with many of the attributes of a growth mindset. They were also considerably more honest and open about their learning behaviour, as evidenced by the way in which they would happily and confidently discuss the aspects of their learning that they found hard for instance.

Final feedback

The final staff meeting was an informal session in which the teachers shared what had worked well for them and areas that they found more challenging or wanted to develop further. We shared ideas and supported each other. This information then fed back into the scheme of work and led to its development.

Stage 3: Continuing development

I have continued to work with staff and refine our approaches to learning and mindsets. The feedback from staff, pupils and parents has had a huge impact on my work and I am indebted to them for their reflections, honesty and support. I have refined the activities and frequently filmed sessions to provide the opportunity to reflect on practice. I have thoroughly researched stories, contexts and stimulus materials to ensure that they provide learning opportunities of the highest quality. I am continuing to refine our ideas and seek new inspiration.

Our recent focus has been on further embedding, challenging and developing the children's understanding of **effort**. These concepts feature in the lessons and also in everyday classroom practice through our use of 'challenge mountains' and explicit and honest discussions about learning. Further details about how to use challenge mountains in the classroom can be found in Year 2 Lesson 5 and Year 3 Lesson 5.

Name: _____   **Date:** _____

What do I think ...?

1. I have a certain amount of intelligence and I can't really change it.

1	2	3	4	5

2. I can learn new things, but I can't change my basic intelligence.

1	2	3	4	5

3. I can change my intelligence.

1	2	3	4	5

4. I can always greatly change my intelligence.

1	2	3	4	5

5. No matter how much intelligence I have, I can always change it quite a bit.

1	2	3	4	5

Tick the correct statement in each box.

Intelligence

☐ I usually think I'm intelligent.

☐ I wonder if I'm intelligent.

New work

☐ When I get new work at school, I'm usually sure I will be able to learn it.

☐ When I get new work at school, I often think I might not be able to learn it.

I would like to work on …

☐ problems that aren't too hard, so I don't get many wrong.

☐ problems that I learn a lot from, even if I don't look smart.

☐ problems that are pretty easy, so I'll do well.

☐ problems that I'm pretty good at, so I can show that I'm smart.

Goal choices

1. If I knew I wasn't going to do well at a task, I probably wouldn't do it even if I would learn from it.

   1   2   3   4   5

2. Sometimes I would rather do well in class than learn a lot.

   1   2   3   4   5

3. It is much more important for me to learn new things in class than it is to get the best grades.

   1   2   3   4   5

4. If I had to choose between getting a good grade and being challenged in class, I would choose (tick one):

☐ good grade   ☐ being challenged

Figure 4 Mindset questionnaire for Year 2 and above, mindsetonline.com, Carol Dweck, 2006

Downloadable resources

PowerPoint presentation for training teaching assistants

PowerPoint presentation for explaining growth mindset to parents

Mindset questionnaire

bit.ly/2dUAQkj

How to use this book

Structure

The lesson plans are organised into year groups and can be followed as a whole-school approach. Each series of lessons has a brief overview that explains where the children are with growth mindset prior to beginning the next series of lessons and what the next set of activities will do to deepen their understanding. You could use this to select an alternative starting point to ensure your children's needs are being met.

The lessons are designed to provide children with opportunities to learn about and discuss the key characteristics of a growth mindset and effective learning. These include:

- learning from mistakes
- failure
- resilience
- perseverance
- challenge
- effort
- self-efficacy.

As these concepts are revisited throughout the school, it deepens the children's understanding and enables them to become confident, independent learners.

The lesson plans for Reception (4–5 year olds) have a different format to the others to ensure that the foundation stage curriculum is fully catered for, including continuous provision. All the lessons begin with a whole-class introduction to the week's focus/stimulus for mindsets. The sessions are designed to be short, involving the children in being active learners, responding to the stimulus and talking to their talk partners. This is then developed further by the use of a group activity and continuous provision. The structure of the Reception lesson plans is discussed in greater detail later in the book.

The lesson plans for Years 1 to 6 (5–11 year olds) all follow a similar structure. They are designed to explore the key concepts within a range of contexts. Often the contexts are flexible and can be adapted to suit the needs and interests of your children. The lessons also contain further developments including ideas for display, follow-up activities and links to supporting materials. The lessons are designed to challenge the children's thinking and include key questions to focus them. In addition, there are challenges to stretch the children's thinking beyond the lesson.

When?

I have explored teaching these lessons at various points in the school year and have found that the most effective time to teach the lessons in Years 1 to 6 is during the second part of the Autumn term and the most effective medium is through Personal, Social and Health Education (PSHE). This allows teachers time to begin to build relationships with the children prior to beginning the mindset journey. In Reception, it is more effective to begin teaching the lessons at the start of the Spring term as this again provides time for the children to settle into school and for the staff to develop relationships with them.

How?

I would recommend teaching all of the six lessons over a half term and in the order they have been written. In Years 1 to 6, you could explore teaching some lessons over more than one session depending on how the children respond and their prior learning. It is important, however, to revisit the concept regularly throughout the school year through informal, open and honest discussion with the children about their learning.

Strategies to use in the classroom

We have listed here a few ideas that you can use in the classroom as you work through the lessons to develop a growth mindset. You probably use many of these strategies already but, if not, they will add to your repertoire. Reminders are given throughout the text on when to use these strategies.

Key language

The lessons introduce the key vocabulary of mindsets and enable the children to effectively describe the characteristics of both growth and fixed mindsets from an early age. This is often done through the use of vocabulary cards which the children are asked to sort. In addition, the books that have been used in certain lessons to support the children's understanding have been carefully selected for their use of the language we wish to promote when developing a growth mindset. At times, it might be useful to include images that reinforce the vocabulary as this will ensure all learners are able to access it.

Some lessons introduce specific language: for example, Year 1 Lesson 5 introduces the word 'persevere' to children within the context of snails and in Year 6 Lesson 1 children are given the opportunity to reflect on the impact of the words we use.

Some lessons also contain examples of children's misconceptions that might occur. Year 4 Lesson 4 includes possible misconceptions and potential strategies for a teacher to help clarify a child's understanding.

Although the language of the classroom is a key element in developing mindsets across a school, it is not my intention to identify key vocabulary for each year group as I would not wish to limit the children's learning. Instead, teachers should build upon and develop the language that the children have been introduced to by being an effective role model.

Teachers as role models

An integral part of the lessons is developing the children's use of language and providing opportunities to talk about learning and so the lessons are rich with language and key vocabulary is introduced and revisited throughout the lessons. But it is essential that this language becomes part of normal class practice and so, as teachers and adults, we should continuously model using it. It is essential that teachers act as role models and are honest and open about their own learning. Through modelling and sharing their own learning journeys, teachers can further develop the classroom culture.

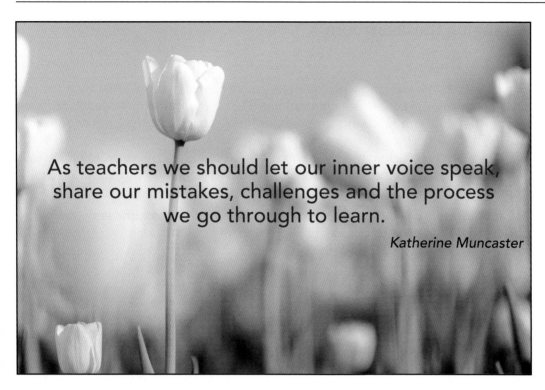

As teachers we should let our inner voice speak, share our mistakes, challenges and the process we go through to learn.

Katherine Muncaster

Teachers as facilitators of learning

The teacher's role within the lesson is often that of a learning facilitator, but adopting this role can initially be quite challenging. It requires teachers to take a step back from being directly involved in the learning for part of the lesson and to listen to the children's discussions carefully without intervening. This will reveal a lot about the children's attitudes to learning and their individual mindsets. It can also provide children with the opportunity to discuss and reflect independently, to listen to different opinions and to resolve issues within their group or with peers. This is an important skill for them to acquire and it also encourages them to develop as independent learners.

During the children's discussions, it is often useful to make a note of the children's responses. This will allow you to share and discuss misconceptions during the feedback or to revisit them at a later point.

Allow the children enough time to discuss each question but not too much time that they become less focused. Monitor the children closely as you want them to remain on task, with their learning moving on. If they have too much time they will become distracted. To ensure the children remain focused, you could use the strategy of 'eavesdropping' where you listen to the discussions from a distance rather than intervening and make a note of the children's ideas. Then, rather than taking individual feedback, you share with the class the ideas you gleaned from listening to the discussions. Ideas can also be shared through a display.

Arranging the classroom

Talk partners

When children are working with their talk partners, it is essential that they are sitting next to each other. The children need to be familiar with working with a talk partner and with following simple rules (for example, taking turns to speak, looking at their partner, talking about the question). Prior to the lesson, you could remind the children briefly of the success criteria for being an effective talk partner, such as the expectations for speaking and listening. This might be done through the use of photographs illustrating the key skills.

The talk partners should be changed regularly to provide children with the opportunity to learn with different children.

If you have children who find it difficult to work co-operatively, you could ask them to talk in a group of three (with at least one member of the group being a good role model).

Small groups

Often the children are required to work in small groups. If it is the first time that they have worked in small groups, you will need to consider the groupings carefully.

Ensure the room is set up to encourage effective discussion between the children. A good arrangement is square tables with the children sitting either side facing each other. The tables could be arranged at a slight angle to ensure everyone can clearly see the board.

To encourage all children to join in the discussion, an object could be passed around the group to indicate turn taking.

Learning groups

The learning groups are designed to provide a clear and coherent structure to group work, which enables children to develop a range of skills in addition to their focus activity. Children must take on one of four key roles: a **manager**, a **reporter**, an **encourager** or a **recorder** (see Figure 25 on page 80). These are designed to be flexible and can be adapted to suit the needs of your class, so roles, for instance, could be shared. Two children could share a role depending on the number of children in your class. The encourager is an ideal role that can be shared.

Initially it is advisable to allocate a specific role to a child and to provide them with a number of opportunities to explore the same role. The children can also wear badges to reinforce the roles they are playing. As children become familiar with this way of working and also more mature, the roles can be changed regularly as this allows them to demonstrate a range of skills.

Prior to using learning groups to develop mindsets in school it would be useful to give the children experience of working in this way. Initially they could be introduced to the different roles and asked to suggest ways in which they should behave or things they should say for each role. These ideas could then be used to create posters to remind the children how to be successful in the different roles. Children should also be given opportunities to practise the different roles. Providing them with opportunities to discuss simple ideas allows them to think more about what is happening in the group and their role. This can then be further developed by activities that require the children to share differing opinions.

The use of learning groups could be developed further by children creating their own success criteria for each role, or the roles could be adapted or extended. For example, the role of a questioner could be introduced which would require the individual to ask questions to clarify meaning and develop ideas further.

When the children are working in roles, it is important for you, the teacher, to act as a facilitator.

Preparing children to give feedback

Once the discussions are over, the teacher's role is to ensure that the children have the opportunity to feed back their ideas and allow other children to respond to them.

You might want to pre-empt any child who could be passive or reluctant to join in by letting them know in advance that you want to hear their ideas. Remind children that there are no right or wrong answers and that you simply want to hear their opinions.

You could also remind the children that you will be randomly selecting them to share their ideas as this will help to ensure they focus. Various methods can be used to select children randomly so that they can give feedback. For example, you could use lollipop sticks where each child's name is written on a stick and one is selected at random. Another useful alternative is to use raffle tickets, where each child has a ticket and the teacher selects a number of a child to feedback or uses a bingo machine to do so. Various online resources are available such as the 'Fruit Machine' at classtools.net or the 'Random Student Selector' at ehyde.com/No%20Hands

In some classes, you might choose to identify a few pairs of children to initially share their ideas with the class and act as role models.

A timer can be used to show the children how long they have to talk for and to ensure they remain focused.

Use of equipment

When using any equipment, ensure these are set up and ready to be used!

It can be very helpful to use a visualiser or document camera to share a reading book with the children. This has the benefit of enabling you to zoom in on specific images to stimulate discussion.

A camera or tablet can be used to take photographs to make cards to show key skills or to add pictures to displays for instance.

Check that YouTube clips and other websites are not blocked in school prior to lessons that include these.

Many of the figures throughout this book give you examples of stimulus to show the children or examples of work by children. You can use these ideas to create your own stimulus materials. However, where you see a QR code, the resources listed are downloadable from the website.

The big picture: a growth mindset culture throughout the school

Whole-school approach

I have worked with a variety of schools to support their implementation of mindsets and the key to their success has been the culture of high expectations for all. The shared vision of every child as a learner – regardless of a child's starting point, ethnicity or home life – is key to successful implementation. It needs to be embodied in the culture of the classroom and staff need to be given time to explore and reflect upon the concept of mindsets. They need to understand and have ownership of it and have the opportunity to review and reflect on classroom practice.

For a whole-school approach to be truly successful, it needs to be led from the top by the head teacher and senior leadership team. This is done best by the senior leader leading whole-school assemblies to reinforce the messages. This book contains three assemblies which explore the characteristics of growth mindset, the desire to be challenged, making mistakes and learning as an incremental process. These can be used at the beginning of each term.

Figure 5 shows the key aspects required for the successful implementation of growth mindsets and a growth mindset culture in a school.

You might begin by directly exploring mindsets through the lessons and activities and this will have an impact on the classroom culture, the language used and the wider life of the school. As this develops, you might find it useful to select an aspect that you feel is a particular focus for your school and explore ways of enhancing this.

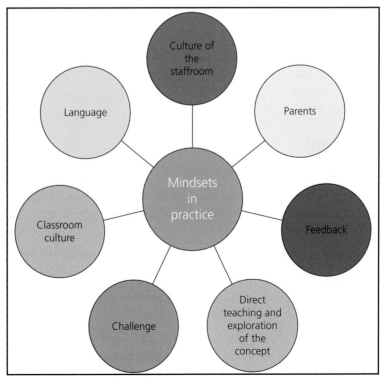

Figure 5 Key factors for successful implementation of growth mindsets in a school

Learning and mistakes

As the culture of the classroom shifts and children become more open and honest about their learning, fantastic opportunities arise to use mistakes as part of the learning journey. At first it is useful to model making mistakes yourself and asking the children to identify them. This could be done by providing the children with opportunities to compare and contrast learning (for example, by asking children to look at two answers to a question in mathematics and to discuss which one is successful and how they know this). Initially the differences will need to be explicit but, as the children become familiar with this, the differences can become more subtle (for example, where a correct strategy is being used but there is an error in the working – see Figure 6).

This strategy is also very effective in developing mathematical fluency, as the successful answer can model how to correctly explain the strategy. This, as well as giving children opportunities to discuss the mistakes of others, opens them up to sharing and discussing their own mistakes. Pupils at my school now explain their thought processes in maths and are extremely honest about them, from sharing strategies to revealing that they have copied someone's work!

Figure 6 Using mistakes in the learning journey

Jo Boaler is an expert on mindsets and maths and I would highly recommend her work (see, for example, Boaler's 2015 book, *Mathematical Mindsets* (ISBN 9780470894521)).

Figure 7 illustrates the importance of mistakes as an integral part of the learning process.

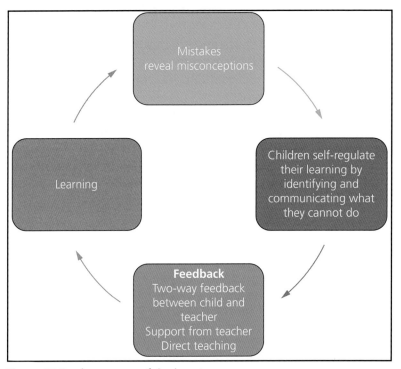

Figure 7 Mistakes as part of the learning process

Feedback and challenge

Dweck emphases the importance of honest and explicit feedback that enables a learner to engage and improve. It is important that, as teachers, we are honest with our feedback and that we identify specific areas of strength and the key next steps. The word 'challenge' is very effective at engaging children in their learning. Initially the teacher should identify a challenge as part of their feedback about a child's learning. The next step, of children identifying their own challenges, then develops this further and can be illuminating. As children become more fluent about learning they can become very specific and subsequently have a huge impact on teaching. Children often identify aspects of their learning that could have otherwise gone unnoticed. At times, the children will even set challenges for the teachers! As John Hattie (2012) says in Visible Learning for Teachers (ISBN 9780415690157), the most powerful feedback is from student to teacher, not teacher to student.

Impact quotes

Ofsted

> ❛The school's strong focus on developing pupils' personal skills and independence through the 'growth mindset' lessons has been significant in developing in pupils a real enjoyment of learning and a confidence to tackle any challenge that they encounter. These skills make a significant contribution to their outstanding achievement.❜

OFSTED Report, 2013

Teachers

'Working together as a staff enabled us to embed the concepts of mindsets across the whole school. Teaching mindsets opens a gateway for children to challenge themselves and learn from mistakes.'

Denise Storey, Year 2 teacher

'Embedding the concept of mindsets in the school culture allows everyone (staff and pupils) to become more effective at challenging themselves and embracing change.'

Frank Earp, Year 5/6 teacher

Children's voice

6–7 year olds

'After learning about the growth mindset I didn't feel scared to put my hand up and ask for help.'

'A growth mindset really helped me improve at maths.'

'Because I know about growth mindset I try to challenge myself.'

'I now love a challenge and want to be the best I can because I understand why having a growth mindset can help me learn.'

10–11 year olds

'A fixed mindset is like being caught in a net.'

'If you have a fixed mindset you'll never be able to do the things you really want to and you'll end up just giving up on what you really wanted to achieve.'

'Growth mindset allows you to make your mark, whoever you are, whatever you want to do.'

'Hold nothing back.'

'If you have a growth mindset, it may take a while, but you will get better and better at what you are trying to do.'

'Having a growth mindset is like drinking a magical potion.'

'I once tried to do something and, after about five attempts, I still couldn't do it but I kept trying and practising and now I can.'

'Growth mindset is vital for learning. Without a growth mindset you could give up on everything.'

'If you have a dream you need a growth mindset to accomplish it.'

'Having a growth mindset can encourage everyone around you to do better at everything.'

'A growth mindset is the way forward. A fixed mindset will never move you along the learning track. If you are fixed you are fixed, if you have a growth mindset you are progressing, growing.'

'With a fixed mindset, I would not be able to overcome tough challenges. Thank you for teaching me the way of a growth mindset.'

'Having a growth mindset helps me learn and develop my brain to the best it can be.'

The future …

From my own experience, the children become the most powerful ambassadors for mindsets, as they develop ownership of their learning and their awareness of the learning process. They begin to challenge their peers, their parents and even staff about learning and this further develops a learning culture in life and a 'buzz' in the classroom and school.

I hope this book inspires you and enables you to develop a learning culture in your school. I would be delighted to hear about your experiences and receive feedback on the ideas and activities. I can be contacted on Twitter @feedyour_brain.

Three assemblies

1: *Zootropolis* – rising to new challenges

Aims

To encourage children to make the most of every opportunity and to rise to new challenges.

Resources

- Bag containing props from the story (a carrot, a police badge, masks for the key characters from the story and a few red herrings)
- Feelings cards (large cards with symbols on including a heart or a facial expression)
- Large speech bubbles
- Whiteboard pen
- Key vocabulary cards: challenge, resilience, persevere, determined
- Suggestions for music (see below) – to be used at any point to reinforce the concept

Assembly

Introduction

Show the children the bag containing the props from the story *Zootropolis*. Explain that the bag contains clues to a story that you want to share with them. State that you will remove an item and take responses from different children predicting what the story might be. Repeat this activity until the children have identified the story.

Ask the children:

Put your hand up if you have seen the film *Zootropolis*.

Who can tell me what the rabbit wanted to be?

Freeze frames

Select some children to use the masks of the key characters and create freeze frames from the story where the other characters are telling Officer Judy Hops that she can't be a police officer. You could have images from the film displayed behind on a big screen during the assembly. Use feelings cards and speech bubbles as visual prompts to explore the following questions:

Ask the children:

What did … say to Officer Hops?

How did that make her feel?

What did she do?

Why do you think she never gave up?

Explain that Officer Hops rose to the challenge and became a police officer. Ask the children to think about a time recently when they have challenged themselves and how they felt and behaved:

Ask the children:

Who likes to be challenged?

Why/why not?

How do you feel when you are being challenged?

What did you do?

Reinforce this with key vocabulary cards: challenge, resilience, persevere, determined.

Explain that we often face challenges in life. These can often be difficult and require us to do our best, persevere and never give up. Just like Officer Hops. To be successful we have to keep trying.

Time for reflection

Close your eyes and take a moment to silently think of a challenge that is ahead of you.

Now, imagine yourself overcoming that challenge.

Imagine that challenge makes you stronger and wiser, and you feel positive that you are going to do your best.

Music

'Try' by Shakira (the theme from *Zootropolis*)

'One more step along the world I go' by Sydney Carter

'It's a new day' (*Come and Praise*, 106)

Follow-up

The masks and story bag could also be used in the classroom to allow the children to role play the different scenarios from the story. Photographs could be taken and these could be used to create a display reinforcing effective learning behaviours and encouraging children to challenge themselves.

In circle time, the children could be asked to discuss how they wish to challenge themselves and teachers could model their own personal experience of challenge.

The story of *Zootropolis* could also be used for an assembly that focuses on inclusion and diversity, by discussing the role of the predators and the prey in the story and how they live harmoniously.

2: Learning from our mistakes

Aims

To encourage children to see mistakes as part of the learning process.

Resources

- A box containing beads or small bricks
- A box wrapped as a present
- A range of objects and images in an open box to represent what you have learned (see Part 3 below)
- Key vocabulary cards: learner, resilience, persevere, determined
- Suggestions for music (see below) – to be used at any point to reinforce the concept

Assembly

Part 1: A mistake

Stand in front of the children with the box containing lots of small things (beads or bricks work well for this as they are small). Accidently drop the box on the floor and allow the objects to spill out. As this is happening ensure you model an upset and worried facial expression.

Provide the children with time to react to the situation: often some children will offer to help, while others may just laugh. Settle the children, ensuring they are ready to listen.

Ask the children:

How do you think I felt when I made the mistake and dropped everything?

How do you feel when you make a mistake?

How should we react when someone makes a mistake?

Part 2: My favourite mistake

Show the children the box wrapped as a present and explain that it contains something very important and special. Ask the children to think about what might be important and special to you and share some of their ideas.

Explain that your favourite mistake is inside the box and that you want to share it with the children. You might wish to have an object or an image inside the box to represent the mistake.

An example of a mistake that you made could be a calculation in maths, for instance 4 + 8 = 10. This could be displayed on a large screen and the children could be asked to reflect upon why you were wrong.

Ask the children:

Why am I wrong with this calculation?

Why do you think this mistake is important to me?

Why do you think I made this mistake?

What caused me to make this mistake?

What do you think I learnt from making this mistake?

Part 3: Learning from my mistakes

Explain that you learnt a lot from making this mistake. Expand on this further by removing examples from the box of the things that you've learnt. These might include:

'I learned that I need to double check my work.'

'I learned that I needed to ask for help if I am stuck.'

'I learned that I need to practise this more.'

'I learned that I need to not rush when I am learning.'

'I learned that I need to use my number bonds to help me.'

You could illustrate the things you learned and display them on a screen or ask a pupil to hold up a poster reinforcing each one.

Part 4: We all learn from our mistakes

Ask the children to think about a mistake that they have made and what they learnt from it. Ask the children:

Who likes to make mistakes?

Why/why not?

Can you tell me about a mistake that you have made?

What did you do?

What did you learn from it?

Explain that we are all learners and that, as learners, we will not be able to do everything straightaway. Tell the children that we should make mistakes as part of the learning process and use them to improve. Making a mistake can often make us feel sad and disappointed, but instead we should see it as an opportunity and continue to do our best, persevere and never give up. Just think about all the things that you are learning in the process. Just like me!

Reinforce this further with key vocabulary cards: learner, resilience, persevere, determined.

Time for reflection

Close your eyes and think about a mistake that you have made.

Think about how it has made you stronger and helped you to develop as a learner.

Now, think about how you will respond next time you make a mistake.

Remember to always strive to do your best and don't be afraid to ask for help to help you improve.

Music

'Try' by Shakira (the theme from *Zootropolis*)

'Sesame Street: Big Bird Sings about Mistakes' by the cast of Sesame Street: youtube.com/watch?v=GHkymY6yKMg

Follow up

The staff could create a display sharing the mistakes they have made and what they learned from them. Examples could include failing their driving test and re-sitting it or falling over when learning to ski and getting back up again so that they could practise more. This helps to reinforce the idea that we all make mistakes and can learn from them.

It is important the staff know the theme of your assembly prior to you sharing this with the children as this will enable them to reinforce it. In lessons, when children make mistakes, the teacher should emphasise through discussion and feedback that they are being learners and should ask the children how making that mistake has helped them to improve.

3: *The Dot* (from small beginnings ...)

Aims

To encourage children to always try when learning new things.

Resources

- *The Dot* by Peter H. Reynolds
- A picture of a large dot
- Two contrasting drawings of people (either displayed on a screen or enlarged to allow all children to see them): one should be a simplistic stickman drawing of a person that has not included all the key body parts while the other should be a more complex drawing of a person (still imperfect but much better)
- Suggestions for music (see below) – to be used at any point to reinforce the concept

Assembly

A dot

Show the children a picture of a dot. This could be displayed on a screen or on a large piece of paper. Explain that you want them to think about whether they would be happy if a child in their class produced this in an art lesson. Once the children have had time to reflect on your question, develop this further by asking the children:

How would you feel if you were the teacher and someone drew this?

What would you say to them?

Can you convince me that this is a 'good' piece of learning? Why do you think that?

The Dot

Read the story of *The Dot* to the children or share it by watching a retelling of the story on the screen.

Once the children have listened to the story, ask them to reflect on it and then take feedback:

How did Vashti feel at the start of the story?

How did Vashti feel at the end of the story?

What helped to change Vashti's behaviour and encourage him to try?

What type of mindset did he have at the beginning of the story?

What type of mindset did he have at the end of the story?

What did Vashti do at the end of the story?

Why do you think he encouraged another child to have a go?

Explain that Vashti was encouraged by his teacher to try to see his dot as the starting point in his learning in art, that he became more confident and willing to try, and that this helped him to learn.

Getting better

Show the children the two contrasting drawings of people. Explain that the drawings were created by the same person.

Ask the children to reflect upon what helped the person to learn how to draw and to improve:

What has helped this child to get better at drawing?

Can you think about anything else that would help you to improve?

What would you say to someone to help them improve?

How would you feel if you were the child looking at your different drawings?

Explain that we can all learn to be better at something but that different things help us to improve. Ask them to reflect upon something they have got better at.

Time for reflection

Close your eyes and take a moment to silently think of a something that you have got better at.

Think carefully about what helped you to improve.

Think carefully about how you can help others to improve.

Music

'It's a new day' (*Come and Praise*, 106)

Follow-up

The children could retell the story with props or small world play. Older children could write a script for *The Dot* or they could create their own versions and these could be shared in a follow-up assembly.

In circle time, the children could be asked to share something that they had improved at and what had helped them to get better at it. These ideas could then be used to create a display that can be acted out as prompts for learning behaviours.

Lessons for 4–5 year olds (Reception, UK)

Lesson		Focus	Page
1	'Help! I'm stuck!'	Different ways to do something tricky; putting your coat on by yourself; feelings when things are difficult	35
2	Everyone can learn to ride a bicycle	Feelings about difficulty; encouraging themselves and others to try again	38
3	Incy Wincy Spider	Identifying challenging things; setting challenges	41
4	Cleversticks	Characteristics of the mindsets; helping a character to have a growth mindset; setting challenges	44
5	Toppling towers	How to tackle difficulty; setting personal challenges; taking risks	48
6	Rooting for you	Identifying challenging things; setting personal challenges	52

Overview

These lessons introduce the concept of mindsets in bite-size chunks. The concept is reinforced through engaging stories. The idea that learning is difficult is explored in a range of familiar scenarios. Children are given the opportunity to experience challenging activities and to begin to reflect on how they felt when they were not initially successful. At the end, the children begin to identify their own learning challenges and to view learning as a journey.

These Reception lessons are presented in a slightly different format to the later lessons to ensure that the Early Years Foundation Stage (EYFS) curriculum is fully catered for, including continuous provision.

Lesson structure

Each lesson begins with a whole-class introduction to the week's focus/stimulus for mindsets. Ideally, the initial whole-class discussion should take place at the beginning of the week as this will allow enough time for the children to access the continuous provision and the group activity during the rest of the week.

These introductory sessions are designed to be short and to involve the children being active learners, responding to the stimulus and talking to their talk partners. The lessons will be more effective if the children are familiar with working with a talk partner and are clear on how to be successful at this (see *Outstanding Formative Assessment*, Chapter 4, by Shirley Clarke).

Group activity

The group activity can be led either by the teacher or another adult. During the small group discussions, it is useful to make brief notes and to keep examples of the children's thoughts and suggestions. One helpful way of doing this is by using laminated speech bubbles together with the child's photograph. See Figure 8 (page 40) in Reception Lesson 2 as an example of how to do this. These can then be displayed as a reminder in the classroom and they will also give individual children ownership of what they have said. Often you will find children reminding others of effective learning behaviours as they follow them around with their speech bubble!

Continuous provision

The continuous provision activities are designed to reinforce the concept and allow the children to explore it independently through small world play, constructions and the opportunity to be creative. The idea of challenge within this is introduced in the lesson 'Toppling towers'. The children are offered different challenges using the visual image of a mountain. The colour of the mountain will relate to the challenge. Gradually, as the children become more familiar with this, they are given opportunities to create their own challenges.

To encourage the children's independence and to ensure they understand the task, an app such as Aurasma (aurasma.com) is very effective. As a QR reader, it allows children to scan an image using a tablet and the code then leads them to a video (that staff or children have uploaded previously) that explains the challenge. The children can then attempt the challenge and can re-watch the instructions at any point. To develop this further the children can begin to explain the challenges that they have set and these can be displayed and uploaded for others to see.

Bringing it together – what have we learned?

This plenary session needs to take place once the children have had access to the different opportunities in the classroom. Again, it is a short session facilitated by the teacher that brings together ideas and challenges learning further.

1 'Help! I'm stuck!'

Learning objectives	Resources
• To identify different ways a person can learn to do something tricky • To identify the steps to success for putting your coat on by yourself • To describe how you feel when learning or doing something difficult	• Teacher's coat • Camera or tablet • Photographs of children putting their coats on • Coats and clothes with fastenings • Mazes • Materials to create mazes • Photographs of mazes

EYFS reference

Effective learning

A unique child

Being willing to 'have a go'
- Seeking challenge
- Showing a 'can do' attitude
- Taking a risk, engaging in new experiences, and learning by trial and error

Playing with what they know
- Representing their experiences in play
- Taking on a role in their play
- Acting out experiences with other people

Keeping on trying
- Persisting with activity when challenges occur
- Showing a belief that more effort or a different approach will pay off
- Bouncing back after difficulties

Lesson

1   *Arrange the children so they are next to their talk partner on the carpet. The children need to be familiar with working with a talk partner and with following simple rules (for example, taking turns to speak, looking at their partner, talking about the question). It would be useful to remind the children of the expectations for speaking and listening through the use of photographs illustrating the key skills.*

Enter the room with your coat on back to front and explain to the children that you are stuck. This will quickly grab the children's attention and stimulate the discussion.

2 Ask the children to talk to their talk partner about:

Why am I stuck?

What is the problem?

You could use a timer to show the children how long they have to talk for and to ensure they remain focused.

Take feedback from a small number of pairs that you select randomly.

3 Model trying to put your coat on in different ways and keep getting stuck (for example, back to front, inside out and upside down). Then tell the children: '**It's too challenging. I just can't put my coat on!**'

Explain that you need the children's help to think of ways to learn how to put your coat on. Ask the children to talk to their talk partner about:

How can I learn to put my coat on?

Listen to the children's discussions and encourage them to think of different ways. It might also be useful to provide some pairs with an object to pass between them to indicate whose turn it is to speak.

Invite the children to feedback their different ideas. Initially, you could ask some pairs that you know have original ideas and would be effective role models. Then select some children randomly.

If the children suggest strategies that are not helping them to learn to do it themselves, then challenge them (for example: '**But I wanted to learn to do it myself. How can that help me?**').

4 During the week, a member of staff could take photographs of the children demonstrating different strategies that help you learn to put your coat on. Alternatively, this could be saved for the group activity and the photographs then displayed.

Group activity

During the week small groups of children should work with a member of staff and revisit the challenge of putting your coat on independently.

Look at the picture of the teacher stuck in the coat. Ask the children to talk to their talk partner about how you can learn to put your coat on.

Once they have shared their ideas, narrow the focus of the discussion to the steps they would need to take to put on their coat. Ask them:

What would be the first thing you would do?

How will that help you?

What would you do next?

You could provide each pair with a coat to model the different steps. This will allow the children to check that their ideas work and are in the correct order.

Within the group, share the children's ideas and, if appropriate, use a tablet to share the children's images and put them in order. Or, if you have already taken photographs, provide the children with a set to put in order to show how to put your coat on successfully. This will create visual success criteria that can be annotated with instructions and displayed in class.

If the children suggest strategies that are not helping them to learn to do it themselves, then challenge them (for example: '**But I wanted to learn to do it myself. How can that help me?**').

Continuous provision

Provide an assortment of different coats or costumes that use a variety of fastenings. The children could be asked to sort them by level of challenge and to choose a challenge. This could be displayed as the weekly challenge activity. The children can then work together trying to put the different costumes on and can record the process using cameras.

Stuck! Draw a maze on the playground and ask an adult to model being stuck in the maze. The children should help the adult to escape the maze by giving instructions and encouraging them. Show the children photographs of mazes if they do not know what a maze is or if further explanation is needed.

The children can then create their own mazes and give instructions on how to get out. Discuss how the children can help you get out of the maze and how they can make it more challenging.

Materials can also be provided for the children to create their own mazes in the creative area. Examples could be given as different challenges for the children to aspire to create or it could be offered as an open-ended activity.

Bringing it together – what have we learned?

This should be completed once everyone has worked on the group activity and when you feel it would have the greatest impact on their learning. The children should be on the carpet with a clear view of the board.

Review the stages of how to put your coat on, using the photographs. Ask the children to help sequence the ideas on the board using the photographs.

Put the photographs in the wrong order and allow the children to correct you. Ask the children:

Is this the correct order?

What is wrong?

What should come next?

Follow-up

Display the strategies for learning to put your coat on independently as a poster to support the children in the classroom.

Repeat the activity for different challenges that the children face, for example, learning to read or using a knife and fork. Use photographs and captions to display the ideas.

2 Everyone can learn to ride a bicycle

Learning objectives	Resources
• To identify how people feel when they find something difficult • To suggest ways of encouraging themselves and others to try again	• Film (or book) of the story *Everyone Can Learn to Ride a Bicycle* by Chris Raschka • Enlarged images from the book • Speech bubbles with the children's photos on them (see Figure 8) • Small world play-bike and costumes • Recording equipment (for example, camera, miniature books, talking tins for voice recording)

EYFS reference

Effective learning

A unique child

Being willing to 'have a go'
• Seeking challenge
• Showing a 'can do' attitude
• Taking a risk, engaging in new experiences, and learning by trial and error

Playing with what they know
• Representing their experiences in play
• Taking on a role in their play
• Acting out experiences with other people

Keeping on trying
• Persisting with activity when challenges occur
• Showing a belief that more effort or a different approach will pay off
• Bouncing back after difficulties

Lesson

1 *Arrange the children so they are next to their talk partner on the carpet. The children need to be familiar with working with a talk partner and following simple rules (for example, taking turns to speak, looking at their partner, talking about the question). It would be useful to remind the children of the expectations for speaking and listening through the use of photographs illustrating the key skills.*

Explain to the children that they are going to watch a story that has no words and that their eyes will have to work extra hard to understand the story.

Watch the film of *Everyone Can Learn to Ride a Bicycle* (with no words). Pause it at **2.05 minutes** OR read the story aloud until the little girl falls off her bike on **page 16**.

2   Ask the children to discuss the following with their talk partner:

How would you feel if you fell off your bike?

Listen to the children's discussions. After a short time bring the children back together and take feedback. Initially you could select particular children to act as role models to share their ideas, and then randomly select others. The children could then be probed further by using these follow-up questions:

Do you think it is easy to learn to ride a bike?

How does the little girl feel when she falls off her bike?

What would you do next?

Would you put the stabilizers back on?

Group activity

The children should work in a small group with an adult.

The children revisit the part of the story where the little girl falls off her bike. You could use the image from page 16 to stimulate the discussion. Ask the children to discuss:

What is happening in the picture?

How does the girl learn to ride her bike?

Once the children have shared their ideas, then develop this further by asking the children to think about:

What would you say to the girl to encourage her to try again?

The children's ideas could be recorded on a speech bubble with their photograph on. This could then be displayed in the classroom as a visual prompt to encourage the children to keep trying.

When all of the groups have completed this activity, the teacher can revisit and share their ideas with the whole class. Re-read the children's suggestions of what they would say. Set them the challenge of trying to use the phrases to encourage others in their learning.

Continuous provision

Stage small world play using figures of a child, a bike and an adult to allow the children to retell the story. This could then be recorded by the children using photographs, talking tins or in miniature books.

Costumes for the different characters and a bike could also be provided for the children to role-play the story outside. Enlarged images could be given to the children to stimulate the activity. An additional adult may also work in role as the child who cannot ride the bike.

Bringing it together – what have we learned?

This should be completed once everyone has worked on the group activity and when you feel it would have the greatest impact on their learning.

Continue to watch or read the remainder of the story. Then ask the children to discuss with their talk partner:

What happens in the next part of the story?

How does she feel when she succeeds?

Next ask the children to feedback their ideas using lollipop sticks or an alternative method to randomly select them. You could remind the children that you will be randomly selecting them to share their ideas as this will help to ensure they focus.

Use further probing questions, if necessary:

What happens next in the story?

What is the girl able to do by the end of the story?

Would the girl have been as successful if she had used stabilizers?

How does she learn to ride her bike?

Model and explain how you felt proud when you had learned to do something and did not give up. You could give a personal example to illustrate this.

Children's responses

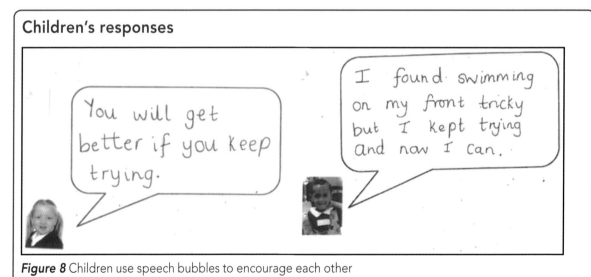

Figure 8 Children use speech bubbles to encourage each other

3 Incy Wincy Spider

Learning objectives	Resources
• To identify things they find challenging • To set challenges for themselves that they can work towards	• 'Incy Wincy Spider' from youtube.com/watch?v=doyv0fL0YJw (or book version) • Picture of the nursery rhyme for the group activity • Laminated sun and clouds • Mark-making materials • Drainpipe • Giant plastic spider • Materials to make spiders (in a variety of colours for the display) • Examples of spiders

EYFS reference

Effective learning

A unique child

Being willing to 'have a go'

- Seeking challenge
- Showing a 'can do' attitude
- Taking a risk, engaging in new experiences, and learning by trial and error

Playing with what they know

- Representing their experiences in play
- Taking on a role in their play
- Acting out experiences with other people

Keeping on trying

- Persisting with activity when challenges occur
- Showing a belief that more effort or a different approach will pay off
- Bouncing back after difficulties

Lesson

1 *Arrange the children so they are next to their talk partner on the carpet. The children need to be familiar with working with a talk partner and following simple rules (for example, taking turns to speak, looking at their partner, talking about the question). It would be useful to remind the children of the expectations for speaking and listening through the use of photographs illustrating the key skills.*

Watch the nursery rhyme 'Incy Wincy Spider'. If you do not have access to YouTube, you could share a picture book version or key images from the nursery rhyme.

2   Ask the children:

What does Incy Wincy Spider keep doing in the rhyme?

Why do you think he keeps trying?

Develop the children's thinking further by posing the question:

Is it easy to keep trying?

Give the children a few minutes to discuss this with their talk partner. During the discussions, the teacher and any other adult should observe and listen to the children's ideas. You could record their ideas to display or to stimulate further discussion.

3   Once the discussions are under way you could choose an opportune moment to extend them further by asking:

Why should you keep trying?

What can stop you from trying?

Randomly select some children to share their ideas with the class.

4   Continue to record their ideas to use on the display, particularly noting things that help you learn and things that stop you learning. These could be displayed on suns and clouds to represent aids and barriers to learning.

Explain that Incy Wincy Spider has a growth mindset as he never gives up and keeps trying his best. Explain that, if you give up, you have a fixed mindset.

Group activity

The children should work in a small group with an adult.

The adults should explain about something that they found difficult (for example, 'I found it difficult to put my head under water when swimming.') They should then develop this further by explaining how they went on to improve and learn how to do it.

It might be useful to compare the adult's learning journey to Incy Wincy Spider crawling up the spout, using an image from the nursery rhyme and referring to it.

Ask the children to share what they find tricky. You could pass an object around the group to indicate whose turn it is to speak.

Develop this further by asking:

How will you challenge yourself and learn to do it?

Create a 3D drainpipe display with the children's spiders and challenges. Inspired by examples of spiders that you show them, the children should make their own spider to climb the drainpipe on the display (see Figure 9).

Place their spiders at the bottom of the drainpipe. As they get better at their challenge they can move themselves up the drainpipe.

Continuous provision

Provide a creative table with materials from which the children can create spiders.

The outdoor classroom could include a plastic spider drainpipe and mark-making materials to allow the children to create different situations for the spider to overcome. The clouds and suns could be written on to show problems and words of encouragement.

Bringing it together – what have we learned?

This should be completed once everyone has worked on the group activity and when you feel it would have the greatest impact on their learning.

Children can revisit the display regularly and, with discussions with staff, 'move themselves up the drainpipe' as they grow closer to meeting their challenge. Initially, you may need to scaffold this for the children, for example: **'Billy has been practising, so he is learning and moving towards his challenge.'** Over time you will find that the children begin to identify for themselves when they need to move and will also begin to remind other children that they are learning and have made progress towards their challenge.

The action of the spider climbing could be used in class as a signal that the children will be doing some challenging things and are in the process of learning.

Children's responses

Figure 9 Moving towards their challenges

4   Cleversticks

Learning objectives	Resources
• To identify characteristics of the different mindsets • To suggest ideas for how a character can develop a growth mindset • To set challenges for themselves and others	• *Cleversticks* by Bernard Ashley • Visualiser or document camera (optional) • Objects to be moved (including dried pasta, beads, cubes, play dough balls, dried lentils) • Containers • Chopsticks • Challenge mountain cards (see Figure 10)

EYFS reference

Effective learning

A unique child

Being willing to 'have a go'

• Seeking challenge
• Showing a 'can do' attitude
• Taking a risk, engaging in new experiences, and learning by trial and error

Playing with what they know

• Representing their experiences in play
• Taking on a role in their play
• Acting out experiences with other people

Keeping on trying

• Persisting with activity when challenges occur
• Showing a belief that more effort or a different approach will pay off
• Bouncing back after difficulties

Lesson

1   Arrange the children so they are next to their talk partner on the carpet. The children need to be familiar with working with a talk partner and following simple rules (for example, taking turns to speak, looking at their partner, talking about the question). It would be useful to remind the children of the expectations for speaking and listening through the use of photographs illustrating the key skills.

➡

Read the story *Cleversticks* until the line 'Why couldn't he be good at something too?'

You could use a visualiser to share the book with the children. You could also the zoom in on Ling Sung's face.

2 Ask the children to think about and then to discuss with their talk partner:

How does Ling Sung feel?

If you feel it is appropriate you could develop the discussions further by asking:

What does he want to be good at?

What is he trying to do?

During the discussions you should 'eavesdrop' on the conversations from a distance rather than intervening and make a note of the children's ideas. Then, rather than taking individual feedback, you share the ideas you gleaned from listening to the discussions with the class.

If you have children who find it difficult to work co-operatively, you could ask them to talk in a group of three (with at least one member of the group being a good role model).

Inform a few children that they will be sharing their ideas shortly. Take feedback from the children on their ideas.

3 Now ask them now to discuss:

How would you feel if you kept trying to do something but couldn't do it?

During the discussions you need to monitor the children closely as you want the children to remain on task and focused, with their learning moving on. If they have too much time they will become distracted.

Bring the children back together and again ask them to share their ideas.

Group activity

The children should work in a small group with an adult.

The adult should continue to read the rest of the story about how Ling Sung has a talent. Then ask the children to discuss the following questions in turn:

How does he feel now?

What does Ling Sung do to help the others?

Do you think we all have a talent?

During the discussions you could pass an object round, such as some chopsticks, to indicate whose turn it is to speak.

Develop this further by giving the children some time with their talk partner and ask them to think and talk about:

How can we get better at things?

Take feedback from the children on how to get better at something.

Continuous provision

Allow the children to free play – set out a table with chopsticks and a range of items which the children should try to move using just the chopsticks. Identify one container as the start and another as the finish. Children should explore moving the objects between the bowls.

They can then set challenges using pictures of the different objects (with Velcro on the reverse if needed) and match them to colour-coded challenge mountain pictures (see Figure 10). This type of colour-coding allows the children to discuss which challenge they have tried. A stopwatch could also be added to the activity to allow children to time how many they can do.

Bringing it together – what have we learned?

This should be completed once everyone has worked on the group activity and when you feel it would have the greatest impact on their learning.

Bring the children back together and ensure they are sitting with their talk partner. Look at the page from the book where the teacher is helping Ling Sung.

Discuss with the children:

Do you think it is a good idea for the teacher to fasten his coat?

What do you think the teacher should do?

You could review the free play with the children and take feedback for which was the most challenging object to move. Ask the children to set a challenge for the teacher and then the teacher should attempt to have a turn.

When modelling, the teacher should model failure and respond using a growth mindset. As the teacher models, he or she should 'thought-shower' (that is, explain how they feel and what they are doing).

Children's responses

Figure 10 Challenges and challenge mountains

Downloadable resources

Challenge mountain pictures
bit.ly/2e9ZryZ

5 Toppling towers

Learning objectives	Resources
• To identify different ways a person can learn to do something tricky • To encourage children to seek and create a challenge for themselves • To encourage children to take risks and engage in new learning	• Picture of two towers (see Figure 11) • Construction materials • Building cards with different levels of challenge (see Figure 12) • Challenge mountains (see Figure 12) • Camera or tablet

EYFS reference

Effective learning

A unique child

Being willing to 'have a go'
• Seeking challenge
• Showing a 'can do' attitude
• Taking a risk, engaging in new experiences, and learning by trial and error

Playing with what they know
• Representing their experiences in play
• Taking on a role in their play
• Acting out experiences with other people

Keeping on trying
• Persisting with activity when challenges occur
• Showing a belief that more effort or a different approach will pay off
• Bouncing back after difficulties

Lesson

Part 1: Easy tower

1 *Ensure the children are sitting on the carpet with a clear view of the board.*
Show the children two pictures of towers on the board (see Figure 11 for an example) and ask them:

What can you see?

How many towers are there? (Children should indicate their responses with their fingers.)

The children should then be asked to look closely at the towers and think about which one is an easy tower and which looks like a challenging tower to make.

The children can share their opinions by a show of hands and their ideas could be probed further by asking for reasons.

Figure 11 Two towers – one easy, one tricky

2 *To ensure that all of the children can see the teacher, it would be useful to rearrange them so they are sitting in a circle.*

Explain that you are going to try to build the easy tower and that it is important to keep looking at the picture as you try to build the tower.

Model building the tower and thought-shower or explain the process, for example: '**I need a blue one next so it is the same as the photograph. This is a bit tricky, as I have to keep looking. How many more do I need?**'

As you build the model, deliberately make errors at times, such as using the wrong colour, and allow the children to correct you.

Once you have completed the tower, ask the children for feedback:

What do you think of my tower?

Have I made the same tower as the picture?

Part 2: Development – challenging tower

3 Introduce the next tower by telling the children that you are now ready for a challenge.

Again, you should thought-shower the process, for example: '**On the bottom I need a red with … because that's what is on the picture.**'

Make a mistake and allow the children to correct you, explain why you are wrong and help you do it again.

Ask the children if the task is too tricky/challenging for you and whether you should give up.

Tell the children you are going to have another try and continue to model the process of building the towers. Continue to thought-shower the process you are going through.

4 Ask the children:

Who thinks they would be able to build the tricky/challenging tower?

Develop this further by asking them to discuss with their talk partner:

What do you think you would do if you tried to build the tricky tower and couldn't do it at first?

Group activity

The children should work in a small group with an adult.

The adult should introduce the 'challenge mountain' as a symbol for when something is challenging and tricky and add it to the picture of the tower (see Figure 12). The different colour mountains represent different levels of challenge and is easily recognisable to younger children. However, it is important to swap the level of challenge you associate with a specific colour each term to prevent children simply choosing whatever task they think will be easy or hard.

Explain that you have set challenges for the children in the construction and that they should try to build them. The children can then explore the challenges and have a go at building them.

Extend this further by the children creating their own challenges and recording them as photographs to be shared with others.

Continuous provision

Continue the use of challenge mountains in the classroom, initially with the construction, and observe how the children behave when faced with a challenge. Does this match up to your opinion of the type of mindset they have?

Later this can then be extended to a range of independent activities.

Bringing it together – what have we learned?

This should be completed once everyone has worked on the group activity and when you feel it would have the greatest impact on their learning.

Look at some of the examples of towers and challenges the children have built over the week. You could prepare some children by warning them that they may be asked to speak in order to ensure they feel confident.

Take feedback from the children:

How did you feel when you were trying a challenge?

What helped you to keep trying?

Did you create your own challenge? What makes it a challenge?

Discuss what the children think a challenge is. Ask them to discuss with their talk partner to deepen their level of discussion.

Children's responses

Figure 12 Challenge mountains and building cards with different levels of challenge

Downloadable resources

Challenge mountain pictures

bit.ly/2ev1m5L

6 Rooting for you

Learning objectives	Resources
• To identify things they find challenging • To set challenges for themselves that they can work towards	• *Rooting for You* by Susan Hood • Speech bubbles • Visualiser or document camera (optional) • Puppet-making materials • An outline of a house and a school

EYFS reference

Effective learning

A unique child

Being willing to 'have a go'
- Seeking challenge
- Showing a 'can do' attitude
- Taking a risk, engaging in new experiences, and learning by trial and error

Playing with what they know
- Representing their experiences in play
- Taking on a role in their play
- Acting out experiences with other people

Keeping on trying
- Persisting with activity when challenges occur
- Showing a belief that more effort or a different approach will pay off
- Bouncing back after difficulties

Lesson

1 *Arrange the children so they are next to their talk partner on the carpet. The children need to be familiar with working with a talk partner and following simple rules (for example, taking turns to speak, looking at their partner, talking about the question). It would be useful to remind the children of the expectations for speaking and listening through the use of photographs illustrating the key skills.*

Look at the first illustration from *Rooting for You*. Ask the children to discuss:

How is the seed feeling?

Why do you think it doesn't want to go out?

You could use a visualiser to share the book with the children. You could also zoom in on specific images to stimulate discussion.

2 Continue to read the next three pages of the story until the line 'all alone' on **page 8**. Ask the children to discuss with their talk partner:

If you were a seed, would you stay in the ground or would you want to go outside?

Remind the children that there are no right or wrong answers, just their opinions.

Once the discussions are underway, you should listen in to the conversations and make note of any interesting ideas. You could identify a few pairs to initially share their ideas with the class and act as role models.

Randomly select children using lollipop sticks to provide feedback on how they would behave if they were the seed. Probe their ideas further by asking:

Why would you behave like that?

What would help you to behave differently?

Group activity

In small groups, finish reading the story and ask the children:

Who helped the seed to keep on trying and growing?

What would you say to the seed to encourage it to keep trying?

Who helps you to keep trying?

Collect some of the children's ideas on speech bubbles as these can be used as visual prompts to remind the children to keep trying.

Continuous provision

In the creative area, leave materials such as socks and pegs for the children to create their own character that is willing to try.

To encourage them to learn to try new things, ask the children:

Can you give your character a name?

How can you help your character to try new things and to learn?

Bringing it together – what have we learned?

This should be completed once everyone has worked on the group activity and when you feel it would have the greatest impact on their learning.

Provide time for the children to share their puppets and feedback on how they help them to learn and try new things.

Discuss who and what helps the children to learn new things in school and at home. Illustrate these on an outline of a house and an outline of a school.

Follow-up

The teacher could model the attributes of both growth and fixed mindsets using a class puppet. We recommend having **a single puppet to model both mindsets** as this reflects what both adults and children do in their learning.

Create a 'have a go board': make a display board of photographs of the children having a go (that is, trying to do something new or challenging). Also ask parents to share examples from home and outside school and display both. This reinforces the idea that mindsets can apply in every aspect of our lives. Staff could also add their own attempts at having a go at new things to the display to model their own growth mindsets.

Lessons for 5–6 year olds (Year 1, UK)

Lesson		Focus	Page
1	I give up!	Characteristics of growth and fixed mindsets; helping a character to develop a growth mindset	56
2	Strictly can't dance	How it feels to fail; how to learn	59
3	Grow, grow, grow your brain	Describing the learning journey; what learning means	63
4	Soaking up the learning	Identifying the characteristics of growth and fixed mindsets; what happens in the brain when we learn	69
5	Super snails 1 – the power of perseverance	The snail's growth mindset; identifying personal challenges	72
6	Super snails 2 – setting challenges	Characteristics of a growth mindset; setting personal challenges	75

Overview

Following on from the Reception activities, these lessons reinforce and explore the concept of mindsets through familiar contexts. They also introduce key vocabulary including persevere and failure. Children work collaboratively with talk partners and small group learning is introduced. The lessons also look at the brain and begin to explore what happens in the brain as we learn. Learning challenges are reinforced and effectively illustrated through the use of snails. Children are asked to begin to consider how they can improve their learning and suggest strategies to support themselves as learners.

1 I give up!

Learning objectives	Resources
• To identify characteristics of growth and fixed mindsets • To suggest ideas for how a character can develop a growth mindset	• Charlie and Lola DVD: *Too Many Big Words* (Series 2, Episode 26) • Giant thought bubble • Giant heart shape

Lesson

1 *Introduce the concept of mindsets using a story with familiar characters. Charlie and Lola works extremely well as the children are familiar with the characters and attracted by the delightful illustrations. The story is about Lola starting school and how initially she enjoys attending until she decides it is too tricky for her. After that, she decides that she wants to stay at home.*
Watch the Charlie and Lola DVD until **4.43 minutes**.

2 Using two children in role as Charlie and Lola, create a freeze frame of the characters sitting together ready to discuss Lola's problem. This can be done using some props, masks and some creative flair. You might find it useful to discuss the roles first. Points for discussion could include:
How would Charlie and Lola freeze?
How can you show how you are feeling using your face and body?

3 Once the children are in their freeze, you can use a giant thought bubble over a character's head to stimulate discussion or a giant heart to represent how a character is feeling.
Ask the children to discuss with their talk partner:
How is Lola feeling?
Why does she feel like that?
Ask the children to feed back. Select pupils to contribute at random, using lollipop sticks or an online resource such as the 'Fruit Machine' at classtools.net or the 'Random Student Selector' at ehyde.com/No%20Hands.
Then allow the children to relate how Lola is feeling to their own experience.
Ask the children:
Have you ever felt like Lola?
What made you feel like that?

Understanding children's mindsets

4 *The children should now work in small groups. If this is the children's first time working in small groups you will need to consider the groupings carefully. To encourage all children to join in the discussion, an object could be passed around the group to indicate turn taking. You might also want to pre-empt any child who could be passive or reluctant to join in by letting them know in advance that you want to hear their ideas (and that there are no wrong answers).*

Ask the groups to discuss:

If they were Charlie, what they would say to Lola?

Once the discussions are underway, you should undertake the role of a learning facilitator. Listen to what the children are saying as it will reveal a lot about their attitudes to learning and their individual mindsets. Try not to intervene since allowing pupils to resolve issues within their group is an important skill for them to develop.

Ask the children:

Why shouldn't we give up?

5 You need to choose the right moment to intervene with an extension activity. This is always tricky, as you do not want to interrupt the children's discussion but need to ensure the learning continues to develop.

Bringing it together – what have we learned?

Invite the children to feed back their ideas for what Charlie should say to Lola and collect them for a display (see Figure 13). Encourage the children to think about each other's ideas. Give them one example of Lola giving up. Ask them if giving up is a good idea or not.

Probe the children further to explain their thinking. Explain that Lola is demonstrating a fixed mindset when she tries to give up and Charlie is encouraging her to have a growth mindset and to keep trying.

Challenge

You could set the children the challenge of presenting their ideas in role as Charlie and Lola. If children are unfamiliar with the idea of a learning challenge, you might want to explain this concept in greater detail, dangling it as a carrot for all children to aim for.

Further developments

Model your own learning and describe a time when you felt like Lola. Describe what you did to overcome the feelings.

Identify times when children are demonstrating a fixed mindset in their learning and encourage them to develop a growth mindset through feedback.

Create a class display board using the children's ideas. This can act as a prompt for the children as to what mindset they should adopt.

Read a story about a character that has a growth mindset. Then use this character as a visual reminder of the importance of persevering. Drop the character into flipcharts, worksheets and instructions.

Children's responses

Figure 13 Encouraging a growth mindset

Downloadable resources

Video of children discussing fixed and growth mindsets

bit.ly/2e3ApT7

2 Strictly can't dance

Learning objectives	Resources
• To describe how it feels to fail • To suggest ways they can support each other and learn new things	• *Giraffes Can't Dance* by Giles Andreae • Visualiser or document camera (optional)

Lesson

1 *Arrange the children so they are sitting with their talk partner and are able to easily see the book.*

Read the story *Giraffes Can't Dance* until the section **on page 12** when all the animals laugh at Gerald. You could use a visualiser to share the book with the children. You could also zoom in on Gerald when the animals all laugh at him at the ball. This will help to focus the children's discussion.

2 Ask the children to discuss:

How is Gerald feeling?

Why is he feeling like that?

Ensure you monitor the children's discussions carefully, allowing them enough time to discuss each question but not too much time so that they become less focused. To ensure the children remain focused, you could use the strategy of 'eavesdropping' where you listen to the discussions and make a note of the children's ideas. Then, rather than taking individual feedback, you share the ideas you gleaned from listening to the discussions with the class.

3 Extend the discussion further by giving the talk partners a few minutes to discuss each of the following:

How do the other animals behave?

How does that make Gerald feel?

What has he failed to do?

Take feedback from different children, act as a scribe or get another adult to jot down words to describe how Gerald is feeling. These could be used for a display to illustrate the learning process from making mistakes.

➡

Understanding the children's opinions on failure

4 *The children should now work in small groups (three to four members). If this is the children's first time working in small groups you might want to consider the groupings carefully. To encourage all children to join in the discussion, an object could be passed around the group to indicate turn taking. You might also want to pre-empt any child who is passive or reluctant to join in by letting them know in advance that you want to hear their ideas (and that there are no wrong answers). You could allocate the name of one of the animals from the story (for example, the 'rockin' rhinos') to each small group.*

The children should then discuss and decide:

Should Gerald be allowed to go to the ball?

Each group should decide if they would let him go and provide reasons for their decision.

Once the discussions are underway, you should undertake the role of a learning facilitator. Listen to what the children are saying as it will reveal a lot about their attitudes to learning and their individual mindsets. Try not to intervene since allowing pupils to resolve issues within their group is an important skill for them to develop. You could make notes of the children's responses to allow you to revisit misconceptions at a later point or share ideas through a display.

5 The children could record their ideas in a 'for and against' format. You would need to ensure, however, that this does not distract from the quality of the discussion.

Bringing it together – what have we learned?

Prepare the groups for feedback time by giving them a five-minute warning to prepare a member of their group to share their ideas. To begin with you could select a confident child from the group but, as the children become more familiar with working in small groups, they could nominate their speaker themselves or more reluctant children could be encouraged to try the role.

The children should then give feedback about their decision: would they let Gerald go to the dance? Ensure you probe the children to explain why they have reached their decision.

Probe the children further by asking them:

Did everyone in your group agree?

How could you encourage Gerald to want to try to join in?

Provide each group with the opportunity to feedback on their ideas.

Challenge

Ask the children to consider awarding a score for the amount of effort the characters put into their dancing.

Ask the children to think about:

Who would you award the most points for effort to?

Which is more important – trying your best or something being easy and getting it right?

Further developments

Expand on this theme by asking the children to think about something they have found tricky to do and how they have got better at it, for example, learning to swim, ride a bike or read.

Create a class display featuring a scene from the ball; include vocabulary to describe how Gerald is feeling after he fails (see Figure 14). Reinforce the concept of learning from our mistakes by displaying comments that the children have suggested about why Gerald should try again and reasons why he should be allowed to go to the ball.

Children's responses

How is Gerald feeling?

'Sad because all the other animals can dance but Gerald can't.'

'Sad because he has been left out.'

'Down and upset as everyone is leaving him out.'

'Left out and upset.'

How do the other animals behave?

'Bad, naughty they are just leaving him out because he can't dance. You shouldn't do that.'

'Just because he can't dance doesn't mean he can't join in.'

'They are laughing at him, saying he can't dance and teasing him.'

Should Gerald be allowed to go to the ball?

'He can come to the dance, we will teach him.'

'He should just try.'

'He shouldn't because the others (animals) might be mean.'

'He should just go to the ball, people shouldn't be mean.'

'He can go, he just needs to practise.'

'If he doesn't go, he won't get better. This could be a problem at a party.'

❛Yes, as if he practises he would be able to learn to dance. You don't just know it, you have to try and learn.❜

❛If you have a go, maybe you can do it. Just try one go.❜

❛If he can't dance, he can't dance.❜

❛No, because he should be able to dance first.❜

❛Yes, as he might get better at dancing there.❜

❛He should go as he might be able to dance. He should ignore the others.❜

Figure 14 Don't give up!

3 Grow, grow, grow your brain

Learning objectives	Resources
• To discuss and share their opinions on what they think the word learning means • To describe the learning journey, using the pictures to support	• Brain cards (see Figure 15)

Lesson

1 *Ask the children to sit with their talk partner.*

Slowly reveal the word '**learning**' on the board. Read the word to the children and ask them to read it to you. To hook the children in, you could read the word in different voices, such as your posh voice or your whispering voice. Ask the children:

What do we mean by the word learning?

Explain that they are going to discuss with their talk partner what they think about or associate with the word 'learning.'

Pre-empt the children by reminding them that there are no right or wrong answers, just their opinions, and you are going to select children to share their ideas randomly, for example, through the use of raffle tickets with the children's names on them.

2 After a short discussion time of a few minutes, bring the children back and randomly select children to feedback to the class about their ideas. When responding to the children's ideas, try to respond in a neutral manner and pose questions to probe their ideas further rather than instantly correcting any misconception.

What does learning look like?

3 Ask the children to sit at tables with their talk partner. Provide each pair with the four different pictures of the brain (Figure 15). Ask them to discuss:

What do you think is happening to the brain in each picture?

Why do you think that?

What does this remind you of?

During the children's discussions, and when you feel it is appropriate, provide brief reminders of their focus. This could be done either as a whole class or to specific pairs to refocus them.

➡

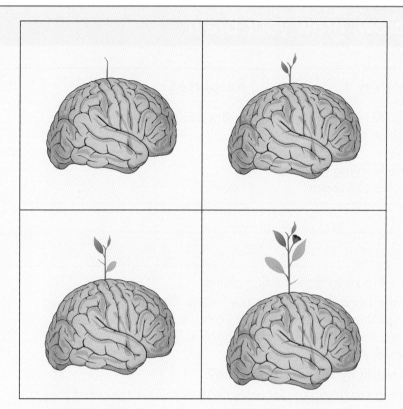

Figure 15 Brain cards

4 Ask the children to feedback what they think is happening in the pictures. Probe their ideas further by asking:

What do you think is happening in the pictures?

Why do you think that?

Have you ever felt like that when you are learning?

5 During this process some children might automatically put the images into an order. If they have not done so, you could probe their thinking further by challenging them to put the pictures in order. Children will respond to this challenge in different ways: most will put the images in a linear order, although a few might form a learning circle. This can be an extremely revealing activity.

Bringing it together – what have we learned?

Look at the images of the brain growing in order and ask the children:

Why have you put the pictures in this order?

Is there any other order or way of presenting them?

Can you describe what is happening to the brain in the different stages?

Can you describe to your partner a time when you felt like that about your learning?

Depending on the children's discussions earlier and their concentration span, you could focus on one of the questions above rather than all of them. Choose carefully, considering which will elicit the most useful information and reinforce the concept of learning as a process.

During the feedback the teacher or another adult could take notes of the children's ideas for each image. This could then be used in a display as a learning prompt. This learning board can be added to as the children's ideas develop and used as a means for the children to self-identify where their learning is at a particular point. Mini versions could also be put in the children's books and used by them to identify where they are in the learning process.

Challenge

Ask the children to think about whether there is another image or object that they could use to describe the process of learning. Develop this further by asking:

Why have you chosen this object/image to represent learning?

Can you explain what would happen if I made a mistake?

Further developments

Teach the children this song to the tune of 'Row, row, row your boat'. This reinforces the idea that learning is a process and a journey rather than instant.

'Grow, grow, grow your brain,

Challenge yourself today.

Listen, practise, double check

And try in every way.'

Downloadable resources

Brain cards

bit.ly/2dmwToF

Children's responses

What does the word 'learning' mean?

> 'It means you have to listen.'

> 'Having fun.'

> 'Learning makes you think a lot.'

> 'Concentrate and watch what the teacher does.'

> 'Learning means if you don't know something, you're going to learn it.'

Should learning be easy?

> 'No, because it means you already know it!'

> 'If you get it wrong, you can try again. You've got to keep on going.'

> 'If you get it wrong, you can try again. If you get it right you've learned it.'

> 'Learning something new is like entering a dark cave.'

How we learn

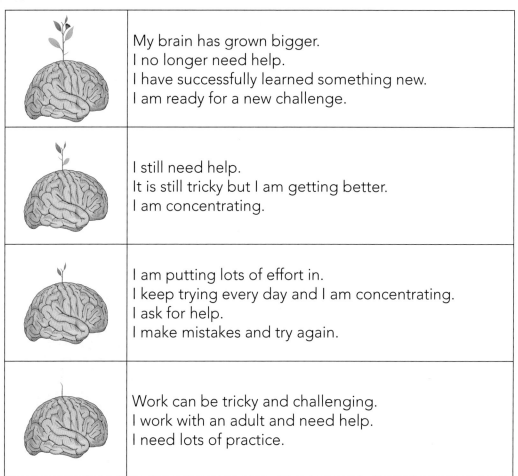

	My brain has grown bigger. I no longer need help. I have successfully learned something new. I am ready for a new challenge.
	I still need help. It is still tricky but I am getting better. I am concentrating.
	I am putting lots of effort in. I keep trying every day and I am concentrating. I ask for help. I make mistakes and try again.
	Work can be tricky and challenging. I work with an adult and need help. I need lots of practice.

Figure 16 Sorting the brain cards (1)

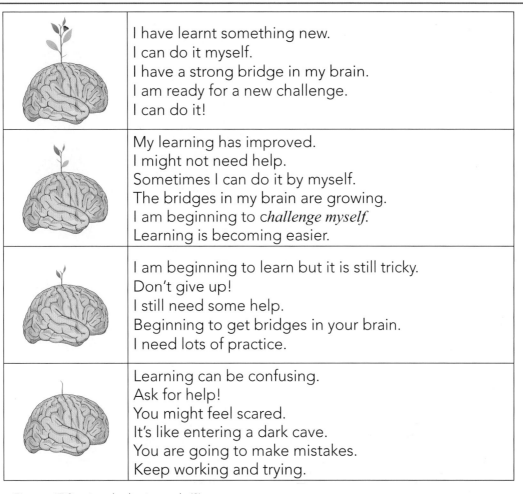

	I have learnt something new. I can do it myself. I have a strong bridge in my brain. I am ready for a new challenge. I can do it!
	My learning has improved. I might not need help. Sometimes I can do it by myself. The bridges in my brain are growing. I am beginning to *challenge myself*. Learning is becoming easier.
	I am beginning to learn but it is still tricky. Don't give up! I still need some help. Beginning to get bridges in your brain. I need lots of practice.
	Learning can be confusing. Ask for help! You might feel scared. It's like entering a dark cave. You are going to make mistakes. Keep working and trying.

Figure 17 Sorting the brain cards (2)

Figure 18 Grow, grow, grow your brain display

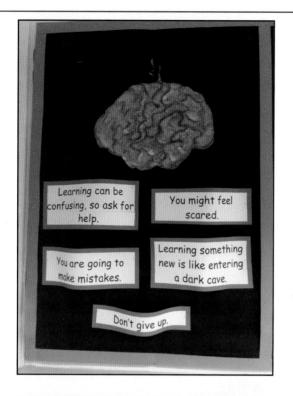
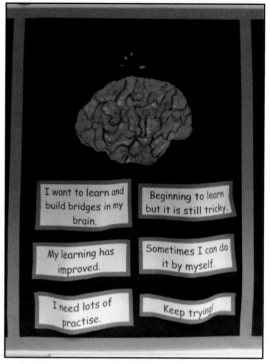
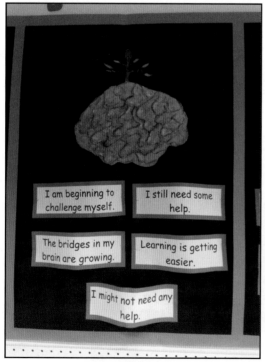

Figure 19 How to grow your brain

4 Soaking up the learning

Learning objectives	Resources
• To identify the characteristics of growth and fixed mindsets • To describe what happens to our brain when we learn	• Two sponge brains (see below) • Laminated labels: 'growth' and 'fixed' • Containers with characteristics and coloured water (see below)

Lesson

1 *Ask the children to sit in a circle.*

Show the children a sponge brain (a sponge that has been cut into the shape of a brain). To distinguish between the two mindsets you could use two different coloured sponges rather than one. Another option would be to place green food colouring in the water in the containers, which represent the characteristics of a growth mindset (see below).

Growing your brain

2 Explain to the children that they are going to help make the brain grow and learn new things. Explain that one brain has a growth mindset and the other has a fixed mindset. Place laminated labels stating '**growth**' and '**fixed**' next to each brain.

Show the children the different containers. Each should be clearly labelled with a characteristic of a growth or fixed mindset:

- giving up
- making a mistake
- trying again
- likes easy work
- doesn't listen
- rushes work
- always likes to be right
- tries a challenge
- keeps practising
- being first to finish
- believes that you can't get better at something

The containers for fixed mindsets should be empty but the ones labelled with the characteristics of a growth mindset should contain water.

In addition to this, you could label some containers with learning behaviours that relate to the children in your class, such as 'shouting out the answers'.

3 Begin by asking the children to sort the containers into growth and fixed mindsets.

Then ask individual children to add possible ingredients to help their brain learn new things and see what happens. The containers containing the characteristics of a fixed mindset should have no effect on the sponge brain. The containers containing characteristics of a growth mindset (that is, those containing water) should be absorbed by the sponge and become heavier.

4 Ask the children to discuss with their talk partner:

What have you noticed?

What has happened to the brain?

Did anything happen when we added the fixed mindset ideas?

Why do you think that was?

Take feedback from the children. Before the children begin their discussion, you could have pre-empted some of the quieter members of your class by informing them that they will be sharing ideas.

Bringing it together – what have we learned?

Pose the question:

Which brain would you rather have? Why?

Discuss this with the children and, if you feel it is appropriate, provide some talk time. Then allow the children to share their ideas and remind the other children to listen carefully as you might be asking them what they think of someone else's idea.

Ask the children:

How can we develop our own growth mindsets?

Challenge

Discuss with the children whether there is anything else we need to make our brain grow and help us to be better learners.

Would you need to have an empty container or one with water in it (that is, a fixed or a growth mindset)?

Display the children's ideas for helping your brain learn new things in the classroom.

Further developments

Challenge the children to identify what they need to do to become a better learner by giving each one a card saying: 'I am making my brain grow and learning by …'.

Create a display entitled 'I am making my brain grow and learning by …'.

Children's responses

Figure 20 What the brain needs to grow and learn

What did you notice when we added the characteristics of the mindsets to the brain?

'The growth mindset brain changed. It's got heavier.'

'The fixed mindset brain stayed the same. Nothing changed.'

Is there anything else we need to make our brains grow?

'Never give up!'

'Go steady.'

'Keep trying.'

'Don't rush.'

'Choose hard work.'

'Listen to the teachers.'

5 Super snails 1 – the power of perseverance

Learning objectives	Resources
• To identify the characteristics of a growth mindset (as demonstrated by a snail) • To identify an aspect of their learning in which they would like to improve or challenge themselves	• A picture of a snail • YouTube clip of a snail at youtube.com/watch?v=Y9yffb7X9fk • Figure 21 or other information about snails • Snail puppet

Lesson

1 *Ask the children to sit on the carpet with their talk partner and ensure they have a clear view of the board.*

Begin by eliciting the children's prior knowledge on growth and fixed mindsets:

What can you tell me about a growth mindset?

What does a fixed mindset mean?

Can you tell me anything else?

If any misconceptions are revealed by the children, you could build in some talk time and ask them to discuss whether they think … is true and why.

Super snails

2 Show the children a picture of a snail and ask them what they know about snails. Select some children randomly to share their ideas with the class. You will need to ensure you move the learning on after a short discussion to avoid the children veering off at a tangent.

3 Explain that they are going to watch a video of a snail and that you want them to think carefully about:

What the snail does

Why the filmmaker chose the music

Watch the YouTube clip of the snail moving to music.

Ask the children to discuss with their talk partner:

What type of mindset do you think the snail has? Why?

How do you know?

Randomly select some children using the lollipop method to answer the questions.

4 Together look at the information in Figure 21 showing some facts about snails and images of snails climbing. You could also show the children a ruler and a timer to illustrate how long it takes and how short a distance snails can travel in that time.

Provide the children with more talk time: ask the children to discuss with their talk partner:

Now you have learned some more about snails, do you think a snail has a growth mindset or a fixed mindset?

Have you changed your original opinion? Why?

Snail facts

Did you know that snails move about 1.3 cm a minute?

They are one of the slowest creatures on the planet.

Snails are very strong. They can lift 10 times their body weight!

Figure 21 Snail facts

5 Introduce the word '**persevering**': write it on the board and read it to the children. Then read it together a few times to reinforce it. Allow the children some time to think about what persevering means. Take ideas from the children and then, depending on their responses, you might need to explain what persevering means. Develop this further by asking the children to think about how the snail perseveres and how they can persevere in their learning. Give the children time to discuss this with their talk partner. To ensure the children remain focused you could use the strategy of 'eavesdropping' where you listen to the discussions and make a note of the children's ideas. Then, rather than taking individual feedback, you share the ideas you gleaned from listening in to their discussions with the class.

Bringing it together – what have we learned?

You will need a medium to large space for this activity: 'Set your inner snail free!'

Invite all the children to curl up into a small ball like a snail inside its shell. Ask them to think about:

If you were a snail, how would you challenge yourself in your learning?

Remind the children that they need to be very quiet and listen carefully to ensure they don't scare the snails! Again, it might be useful to pre-empt a few children, informing them that they will be sharing their challenge with the class. Ask an individual snail to uncurl while sharing how they would challenge themselves. Repeat until all the snails have shared their challenges. Another adult could make a note of the children's individual challenges for the next lesson.

Challenge

Ask the children to think of other animals that they think demonstrate a growth mindset. Can they explain why they think this?

The children could use books or the internet to find out more about animals and their characteristics.

Further developments

Use a snail puppet to represent and reinforce the concept of persevering. When you observe a child persevering in his or her learning, place the puppet next to them, or ask other children to place the snail when they observe another child persevering.

Ask the children:

Are you persevering like a snail?

The idea of snails persevering was the key plot in the film *Turbo-Racing Team*. This can be a useful means of reinforcing the concept, as can the beautifully illustrated book *Snail Trail* by Ruth Brown. There are also a number of great non-fiction books about snails including, *Snails* by Susanna Davidson.

Downloadable resources

PowerPoint presentation 'Snail facts'
Video of children pretending to be snails
bit.ly/2dODsTO

6 Super snails 2 – setting challenges

Learning objectives	Resources
• To explain what a growth mindset is • To identify and set a learning challenge for themselves	• Photographs of snails • Model snail and learning track (see Figure 22) • Photographs of snails • Materials to make snails • Visualiser, document camera or tablet

Lesson

1 *Ask the children to sit with their talk partner. Prior to the lesson, you could remind them briefly of the success criteria for being an effective talk partner.*

Write this question on the board and read it together, using snail photographs to stimulate the discussion where needed:

Do snails have a fixed mindset?

Ask the children to discuss with their talk partner whether they think this is true or false and why. Ensure you monitor the discussion carefully, providing enough time for the children to share their opinions but not too much that they go off task. To prepare the children to share ideas you could to give them advance warning during their discussions that you will be asking for their opinions.

2 Bring the children back together and ask the children to vote on whether they think it is true, false or they didn't know, using a simple thumbs up, down and wavering in the middle method. Select children with different opinions to explain why.

Super snails

3 Recap on the snail and its growth mindset by asking the children:

Which animal did we talk about last week (Lesson 5)?

What can you tell me about a snail?

Can you explain what type of mindset a snail has?

4 Using a visualiser, document camera or tablet, share with the children your snail on its learning track (see Figure 22). Explain you have set yourself a challenge of … that you are going to work towards. Try to pick a personal challenge and one which the children would relate to, such as putting your head under water when swimming or trying to slow down and take more care with your learning. You could share a few examples to ensure the children do not focus on your (single) challenge and adopt it.

Try to use the term 'learning' when talking about your challenge rather than 'work' as it has meaning in a wider range of contexts and is more of a continuous journey that we are on rather than an end product that was laborious.

Model for the children:

- what you were learning to do
- the challenges you faced
- how you overcame the barriers.

Figure 22 A snail on a learning track

5 Explain to the children that they are going to make their own snail and learning track and set themselves a learning challenge to work towards. Remind the children that the challenges might be different, as we are all different learners. Then the children should create learning tracks and snails (to represent themselves). The learning challenge could be written on a sign as the finish line.

You might need to set aside additional time to complete this activity as it can be quite time consuming. You could then have the discussion with their talk partner and plenary later on in the day or week, once all the learning tracks have been completed.

Bringing it together – what have we learned?

Ask the children to share their learning track with their talk partner and to discuss:

What are your challenges?

What strategies can you use to move on your learning track?

How can you get better at this?

What would you need to do?

Can you think of anything that might stop you from moving on your track?

When it is appropriate, take pit stops for the children to feedback about a question and then move the discussion on to the next aspect.

Challenge

Ask the children to think about barriers to their learning. You might want to model your own again here, such as worrying about opening your eyes under water.

What could be a barrier to your learning challenge?

How would you create this on your learning track?

Further developments

Display the learning tracks in the classroom. Then the children can move their snails forwards when they believe that they have demonstrated they are working and improving at their challenge. New challenges can be added also.

Emphasise that it is not a race against others and those who have chosen a harder personal challenge will take longer and are actually working harder! The circular nature of the track reflects how learning keeps moving on.

Children's responses

Figure 23 Child's snail ready to start on its learning track

Figure 24 How snails learn!

Lessons for 6–7 year olds
(Year 2, UK)

	Lesson	Focus	Page
1	Playing teacher	Working in specific roles in a learning group; strategies that would help a child with a fixed mindset engage in their learning	81
2	'Oh no! I've made a mistake!'	How we feel when we make a mistake; strategies which help us learn	84
3	'Girls can't do that!' Dream big!	Debating whether girls should be allowed to be engineers; identifying how we should respond to a mistake	88
4	Super effort	Creating a character to represent effort; the characteristics of effort	91
5	Challenge mountains	Setting learning challenges; reviewing their challenge and identifying progress	99
6	Ding ding! How much effort?	Different stages of effort; creating their own effort meter	103

Overview

From Year 2 onwards children are required to work collaboratively with others through the introduction of 'learning groups'. This builds on from Year 1 where the children worked with a talk partner, as they are now required to work in groups of four and to take on a specific role within the group. Children are provided with opportunities to debate ideas and share different opinions. The idea of mistakes as part of the learning process is explored in greater detail and children are encouraged to identify strategies to enable them to learn. The concept of effort is introduced and the children are encouraged to reflect on their own effort and their desire to be challenged.

Learning groups

The learning groups are designed to provide a clear and coherent structure to group work, which enables children to develop a range of skills in addition to their focus activity. Children must take on one of four key roles: a **manager**, a **reporter**, an **encourager** and a **recorder** (see Figure 25). These are designed to be flexible and can be adapted to suit the needs of your class, so roles, for instance, could be shared. Initially it is advisable to allocate a specific role to a child and to provide them with a number of opportunities to explore the same role. As children become familiar with this way of working and also more mature, the roles can be changed regularly as this allows them to demonstrate a range of skills.

Prior to using learning groups to develop mindsets in school it would be useful to give the children experience of working in this way. Initially they could be introduced to the different roles and asked to suggest ways in which they should behave or things they should say for each role. These ideas could then be used to create posters to remind the children how to be successful in the different roles. Children should also be given opportunities to practise the different roles. Providing them with opportunities to discuss simple ideas allows them to think more about what is happening in the group and their role. This can then be further developed by activities that require the children to share differing opinions.

When the children are working in roles, it is important for you, the teacher, to act as a facilitator. Listen to what the children are saying as it will reveal a lot about their attitudes to learning and their individual mindsets. Try not to intervene since allowing pupils to resolve issues within their group is an important skill for them to develop. This allows them to develop as independent learners. You could make a note of the children's responses to allow you to revisit misconceptions at a later point or to share ideas through a display.

The use of learning groups could be developed further by children creating their own success criteria for each role, or the roles could be adapted or extended. For example, the role of a questioner could be introduced that would require the individual to ask questions to clarify meaning and develop ideas further.

Manager

Their role is to:
- make sure everyone understands
- keep the group on task
- be fair
- ensure the work is completed and decisions are made.

Reporter

Their role is to:
- share the findings of the group with others
- speak clearly and confidently
- read through and organise their ideas.

Encourager

Their role is to:
- make sure everyone joins in
- reward and praise people
- be positive
- increase the confidence of the other group members.

Recorder

Their role is to:
- record the ideas of the group
- suggest ways of wording ideas
- read through and check work
- make sure they record everyone's ideas.

Figure 25 Roles in learning groups

1 Playing teacher

Learning objectives	Resources
• To work in a specific role in a learning group • To identify strategies that would help a child with a fixed mindset engage in their learning	• Picture of a grumpy frustrated child, 'Sara' • Cards or posters explaining learning group roles (Figure 25 on page 80) • Role badges showing 'manager', 'reporter', 'encourager', 'recorder'

Lesson

1 *Arrange the children so they are sitting with their talk partner, either on the carpet or at desks.*

   Introduce the concept of mindsets using the familiar context of school and a fictional child, Sara, being reluctant to learn. Children will relate to some of the behaviours and the feelings that this fictional character displays.

   Introduce the character Sara to the children using an image of a grumpy frustrated child. Depending on your class and the behaviours they display, you could change the gender and the name of the character so that it clearly reflects their needs.

   Explain who Sara is and how she behaves, for example: '**This is Sara. She is a new child who will be coming into Year 2 shortly. However, Sara doesn't like school and can misbehave in class.**'

2 Develop this further by sharing some more information about Sara. Explain that she:
   • refuses to do the work in class
   • moans and makes silly noises
   • says everything is easy so she won't bother
   • bangs equipment and fiddles with pencils
   • tries to distract others
   • shouts out and disrupts lessons
   • grumbles 'I hate Maths/English!'

   You could just focus on some of these behaviours or you could adapt some of them to better reflect the nature of the children in your class.

3 Ask the children to discuss Sara with their talk partner:
   What type of mindset does Sara have?
   Why do you think that?
   Ask the children to feedback to the class and carefully probe the reasons for their opinions.

Playing teacher

4   *The children are now going to work in learning groups. Ensure your room is set up to encourage effective discussion between the children. An effective arrangement is square tables with the four children sitting two either side facing each other. The tables could be arranged at a slight angle to ensure everyone can clearly see the board.*

Explain to the children that they are now going to work in learning groups, with each individual playing a specific role: **manager**, **reporter**, **encourager**, **recorder**. Introduce the group roles to the children using cards or posters as shown in Figure 25 on page 80. If children have already explored these roles when completing a simple task, they will have become familiar with what their job entails.

Allocate a role to each child. Two children could share a role depending on the number of children in your class. The encourager is an ideal role for sharing. The children can also wear badges to reinforce the roles they are playing.

5   The children should then discuss their ideas about the following question as a small group, working in their allocated role:

If you were Sara's teacher, what would you do to encourage her to join in more with her learning?

Once the discussions are underway, you should undertake the role of a learning facilitator. Listen to what the children are saying as it will reveal a lot about their attitudes to learning and their individual mindsets. Try not to intervene since allowing pupils to resolve issues within their group is an important skill for them to develop. This allows them to develop as independent learners. You could make a note of the children's responses to allow you to revisit misconceptions at a later point or share ideas through a display.

It is beneficial to give the children time warnings to ensure they remain on task and to allow the reporter to prepare to speak and share the group's ideas.

Bringing it together – what have we learned?

Prepare the groups for feedback time by giving them a five-minute warning to prepare the reporter to share the group's ideas. To begin with, you could select a confident child for that role within the group but, as the children become more familiar with working in role, more reluctant children could be encouraged to try the role. Remind them that you will be expecting them to share:

What would you do as Sara's teacher to encourage her to want to be a learner?

Why do you think that would be an effective strategy?

Following the five-minute preparation time, the reporter should then give feed back on their group's discussion. Provide each group with the opportunity to feed back their ideas.

Probe the children's thinking and encourage other members of the group to participate. Ask them to explain why they think their idea would be effective. Ensure you probe the children to explain why they have reached their decision and ask them:

Did everyone in your group agree?

Can you see any problems with their ideas?

Challenge

Ask the children to discuss if they have ever felt like Sara and what caused them to feel like that. Thinking back to that time, could they have behaved differently?

Further developments

A follow-up discussion could be based on whether they would allow a child with a fixed mindset to attend their school. Again, the children could debate this within their learning groups.

To continue to develop the quality of the groups' interactions and roles, you could develop success criteria for each role. Two adults could model successful and unsuccessful group roles. The children could observe the interaction and discuss the differences and provide feedback for the adults in order to generate success criteria.

Children's responses

If you were Sara's teacher, what would you do to encourage her to join in more with her learning?

'Give her a special seat with a friend who would show her what effort looks like.'

'Let her do fun things and enjoy her learning.'

'She needs to try her best and challenge herself!'

'Don't give her easy work – she needs to challenge herself.'

'When I first started Reception I was nervous.'

'She should ask for help.'

'The teacher should tell her she will lose her golden time if she doesn't try hard.'

Downloadable resources

Roles in learning groups – cards
bit.ly/2dLNp28

2 'Oh no! I've made a mistake!'

Learning objectives	Resources
• To identify and describe how we feel when we make a mistake • To identify strategies which can help us to learn	• *The Girl Who Never Made Mistakes* by Mark Pett and Gary Rubinstein • Visualiser or document camera (optional) • Picture of the deep, dark learning hole (see Figure 26)

Lesson

1   *Arrange the children so they are sitting with their talk partner and have a clear view of the board and the teacher.*

Show the children the following words, read them to the class and then ask them to read them together with you: **'mistake'**, **'error'**, **'incorrect'**, **'wrong'**.

Before they begin the discussion, remind them that you will be selecting children randomly to share their ideas. Ask them to discuss with their talk partner what the words mean and take feedback from them using lollipop sticks.

2   Read the story *The Girl Who Never Made Mistakes* until Beatrice makes a mistake at the talent show on **page 23**. You could use a visualiser to share the book with the children.

Look carefully at the picture of Beatrice on stage after everything has gone wrong. Zoom in on her facial expression to focus the children's attention. Ask the children to discuss:

How does Beatrice feel?

Why does she feel like that?

What would you do if you were Beatrice?

You could display the key questions for discussion on the board to allow the children to focus their discussions.

Take feedback from different children and act as a scribe or ask another adult to jot down the children's opinions and ideas. These could be used for a display to illustrate learning from mistakes.

The deep dark learning hole

3   Show the children the picture of the deep dark learning hole and explain that often, when we have made mistakes, we feel as if we are stuck in a 'learning hole'.

Explain to the children that they are going to think of ways to help Beatrice and others out of the learning hole and record their ideas on paper.

If appropriate you may want to give guidance for the children to focus their learning. This could be displayed on the board and include:

What would you say?

What could you do?

Who could help you?

How could you represent that in a picture?

You could provide the children with some talk time with their talk partners before they begin working individually to record their ideas.

The deep, dark learning hole

Figure 26 The deep, dark learning hole

Bringing it together – what have we learned?

Perhaps using a visualiser, share examples of the children's ideas and ask them:

Can you share your drawing with the class?

Why have you drawn that?

What does it represent?

How would you feel if you made a mistake like Beatrice and were stuck in the deep dark learning hole?

Challenge

Challenge the children to think about:

What can cause you as a learner to enter the learning hole?

Is there anything specific you can do to help yourself get out of it?

Think about an occasion when you thought you were in the learning hole in school:

How did you feel?

Did you try to get out of it?

What did you do?

Did anyone help you?

Further developments

Use the children's ideas to create a large learning hole display. Show the different strategies represented with a visual prompt as well as words, for example, a ladder. The display can act as a visual reminder for learners and for both children and teachers to use during the learning in the classroom.

Give the children some talk time to discuss:

How can teachers support learners in overcoming their mistakes?

Downloadable resources

PowerPoint presentation 'The deep, dark learning hole'

Video of children deciding how to get out of the deep, dark learning hole

bit.ly/2dYRo9N

Children's responses

Figure 27 Don't panic!

Figure 28 Helping someone out of a learning hole

Figure 29 Getting out of the learning hole

3 'Girls can't do that!' Dream big!

Learning objectives	Resources
• To discuss and debate whether girls should be allowed to be engineers • To identify how we should respond to a mistake	• *Rosie Revere Engineer* by Andrea Beaty • Visualiser or document camera (optional)

Lesson

1 *Arrange the children so they are sitting with their talk partner and have a clear view of the board and the teacher.*

Show the children a picture of the character Rosie from the book *Rosie Revere Engineer*. Ask the children to think about what things the character Rosie might be successful at.

Before they begin the discussion, remind the children that you will be selecting children randomly to share their ideas. Ask them to discuss with their talk partner and take feedback from them using the lollipop sticks. Probe the children's answers further by asking:

Why do you think that?

Dream big!

2 Read the story until **page 12**, where Rosie decides to keep her dreams of being an engineer to herself. You could use a visualiser to share the book with the children.

Explain that Rosie wants to be an engineer but some people do not believe girls can be engineers. Ask the children to initially discuss with their talk partner:

What do you think an engineer does?

After allowing the children a few minutes to discuss it, take feedback and clarify the different things an engineer does. You could also display images of different types of engineers at work to reinforce the concept.

3 Once the children understand what an engineer does, ask the children to discuss with their talk partner:

What are the reasons why Rosie (a girl) could or couldn't become an engineer?

If appropriate you might want to give guidance for the children to focus their learning. This could be displayed on the board and include:

Can you think of any reasons why a girl shouldn't be an engineer?

How would you encourage Rosie to become an engineer?

Can girls and boys do any job they'd like?

Initially, ask the children to share their opinions by a quick poll on whether they think Rosie could or could not be an engineer. Then take feedback from the children and probe their ideas further by asking:

Why do you think that?

Do you need to be good at something to do it?

4 Continue to read the story to the children until **page 26**. Re-read the line: 'The only true failure can come if you quit.'

Ask the children to talk to their partner:

What happened at the end of the story?

Why did her Aunt describe her invention as 'Your brilliant first flop was a raging success'?

Why is something that went wrong still a success?

Bringing it together

Ask the children:

Now you've read the whole story, do you still believe that girls can/can't be engineers?

Take feedback from individual children and, if appropriate, ask other children to comment on these ideas.

You could share photographs of men and women doing jobs that are not stereotypical, including being an engineer or a male nurse, to reinforce the fact that men and women can do any job they wish. There are no limits to what the children can become, whatever their gender.

Challenge

Use the word **FLOP** as a stimulus for the children to create an acrostic, which could act as a learning prompt. You could give the children an example and then ask them to create their own. For example:

First

Learning

Often

Practise

Further developments

Ask the children to think about what they would like to be when they are older. Encourage them to dream big and to draw themselves in the future in their chosen career.

Links to other activities to support this book: andreabeaty.com

Children's responses

What could Rosie be good at?

'Ballet'

'Doing hair'

'Helping people'

'Playing with animals'

'Looking nice'

'Handwriting'

What is an engineer?

'They make things like a car.'

'They fix things.'

'They invent and make things.'

Should Rosie (a girl) be an engineer?

'She shouldn't be an engineer as she gets so sad when things go wrong.'

'She can as boys and girls can do the same thing.'

'Girls and boys can do what they want if they put their minds to it.'

'We think Rosie should be an engineer as she is good at making things.'

'No, because men normally get that job.'

'Boys and girls can get any job if they work hard and practise.'

'She shouldn't be an engineer as she is too nervous.'

'Being an engineer is not just a job for boys!'

'Yes, because she makes fantastic inventions.'

'Yes, because she has tried hard.'

'In the olden days, a girl wouldn't be one.'

'Rosie needs to talk to people and see if they would let her be one.'

How would you encourage Rosie to try?

'Tell her what she is good at.'

'Say never give up!'

'Tell her if you work hard at school you can do it!'

'Keep up your work.'

'Tell her not to listen to the grumpy uncle, he's just being mean.'

Acrostics for FLOP

Failing	**F**antastic
Learning is an	**L**earning
Option so	**O**nly if you
Persevere	**P**ersevere

4 Super effort

Learning objectives	Resources
• To create a character to represent effort • To explain what the characteristics of effort are	• Growth and fixed mindset vocabulary cards (Figure 30) • Wanted poster template (Figure 31) • Visualiser or document camera (optional)

Lesson

1   *Arrange the children so they are sitting with their talk partner. The talk partners should be changed regularly to provide children with the opportunity to learn with different children.*

Give the children key vocabulary cards with words connected to growth and fixed mindsets (see Figure 30).

You could personalise some of the statements so that they reflect behaviours which are specific to your class.

Ask the children to read the words with you and then to you. Ask them to work with a talk partner and to sort the vocabulary into groups. Explain that there is no right answer and you are just interested in their different ideas.

If the children are struggling with any of the words, build in some talk time to discuss and clarify their meaning.

gives up	keeps trying to learn new things	chooses easy work	chooses tricky work	practises
perseveres	tries again	wants to be seen as clever	finds a new strategy to help them learn	likes being first to finish

Figure 30 Growth and fixed mindset vocabulary cards (1)

2   Ask the children to feed back their ideas on how they have sorted the cards:

How have you sorted your vocabulary cards?

What connections have you made?

Could you add any other words or phrases to your group?

Has anyone sorted them in a different way?

It would be useful to display the vocabulary cards on the board or via a visualiser as it will help illustrate the children's ideas clearly.

Wanted: Super Effort!

3 Explain that you want the children to create a character to represent 'Super Effort' when they are learning.

Ask the children to discuss with their talk partner:

How does someone demonstrating super effort behave?

How could you represent that using a character or a person?

What sort of learner would they be?

What might they look like?

You could display these questions as a visual prompt on the board and then, as the children's discussion develops, you could reveal the next question to focus on when appropriate. It is important to be responsive to your children's discussions and to continue to move the learning on.

4 Ask each child to complete a wanted poster for the character 'SEF' and to describe how the character behaves (see Figure 31).

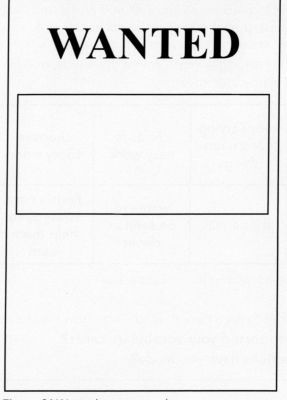

Figure 31 Wanted poster template

Bringing it together – what have we learned?

Provide the children with a few minutes to prepare themselves to share their ideas. Explain to them that you are going to randomly select children to share their wanted posters for SEF and ask them to explain the characteristics of SEF.

Explain to the children that you are interested in:

Why have you represented/drawn SEF in this way?

How does he or she behave?

What would you do if you found learning challenging?

Provide the children with a few minutes to think through their ideas and explanations before using lollipop sticks or an alternative method to randomly select who will respond.

Challenge

Ask the children to write instructions on 'How to behave like SEF' or 'How to be a learning Ninja' (see Figures 34–37).

Further developments

The children could create wanted posters for NEF (No Effort) for crimes against learning and include characteristics of poor learning behaviour.

Select a version of SEF to adopt as a class, create a class puppet and use it as a visual reminder of effective learning behaviours. Display the wanted posters as a reminder of the expectations for learners.

Downloadable resources

Growth and fixed mindset vocabulary cards
Wanted poster template
bit.ly/2d9h0Dp

Children's responses

One child created the idea of a 'learning Ninja' in response to the SEF activity. This led to a great whole-class discussion on how a learning ninja behaves. The children identified a range of characteristics and this had a profound effect on the culture of the classroom. Children would remind each other to behave like a learning Ninja and would praise each other for displaying the effective characteristics. Occasionally, they would even remind me!

Figure 32 Advert for a learning ninja

Figure 33 Wanted: Super Effort for learning

How to be a learning Ninja.

You will need:

Your best behava

a groth mindset never give up

a sharp pencel.

Happy to make marvalent mestakes

what to do:

1. Sit on the Carpet and lern about stuth like maths, English, french, Jerman and Englooh.

2. Ensor you get your learning ninja tools that incloods perservering, a groth mindset, your best Behava and happy to make maverlas mistack.

Figure 34 How to be a learning ninja (1)

How to be a learning Ninja

You will need!
your brain
your growth mindset
your realy good lising eas
1. Ewhen you gre rh on the it is and to lseh to the teecher!
2. Make shor you have your growth mind set (becouse your brain will grow)
3. Behaive nicly so you dont go on the grumpy bord!
4 Only have your mowth open at

Figure 35 How to be a learning ninja (2)

plaitime. 5 Awals have your brain redy to leth. 6. Never give up even if its hard work!

Figure 36 What you need to be a learning ninja

Figure 37 SEF display

5   Challenge mountains

Learning objectives	Resources
● To set a learning challenge ● To review their challenge and identify their progress	● Picture of a mountain (Figure 38) ● Photographs of each child with a speech bubble (see Figure 40) ● Display board showing a giant challenge mountain (see Figure 39)

Lesson

1   *Arrange the children so they are sitting with their talk partner and able to clearly see the board.*

Slowly reveal an image of a mountain (see Figure 38). It might be useful to use a spotlight tool to slowly reveal the image and hook the children. You can then ask:

What do you think this is a photograph of?

Why do you think that?

Ask the children to discuss the following questions with their talk partner:

What can you see?

Would you like to climb the mountain?

How would you feel?

Ask the children to feed back (select pupils to contribute at random, using lollipop sticks or an online resource such as the 'Fruit Machine' at classtools.net or the 'Random Student Selector' at ehyde.com/No%20Hands.)

Figure 38 A giant mountain

2 Develop the discussion further by posing the question:

How is learning similar to a challenging mountain?

Allow the children some thinking time and then ask them to discuss the question. During the discussions, you should use the strategy of 'eavesdropping'. This is where you listen to the discussions and make a note of the children's ideas. Then rather than taking individual feedback, you share the ideas you gleaned from the discussions with the class.

It might be necessary for you to make explicit the link between learning and climbing a challenging mountain. You may need to explain that learning is like climbing a mountain: it can be challenging and you need to practise and have help to overcome the difficult parts.

Challenging myself!

3 Show the children the small pictures of themselves with speech bubbles attached. Ask them to think about:

How can you improve as a learner?

What challenge would you set yourself?

It might be useful to model to the children how to phrase a learning challenge. For instance, you could use pictures of members of staff with their learning challenge written in a speech bubble. It is also extremely effective to use fictional characters that the children are familiar with: Horrid Henry, for example, would have the challenge of being willing to try to have a go at his learning.

Ask the children to set their own learning challenge, identifying a learning behaviour that they wish to improve. The children should then write this on their speech bubble (see Figure 40).

Bringing it together – what have we learned?

The children place themselves on the whole-class challenge mountain (see Figure 39). As or when they feel (or the teacher feels) they are making progress, they should move up the mountain.

Ask the children to talk to their talk partner about what will help them to improve and move up the mountain and what might prevent them from learning.

Once the children reach the top of the mountain, they could set themselves a new challenge and discuss what helped them to improve.

Challenge

Ask the children to think about their learning challenge and to create 'steps for success' by breaking down the steps they need to take to achieve it.

Further developments

Using Adobe Spark Video (spark.adobe.com), which is free to download, the children could review their learning and create a short film using photographs of their work before and after it has improved, with a voiceover explaining how it happened.

Ask the children if they can think of another image or method of explaining learning.

How would they illustrate this?

Children's responses

Figure 39 The challenge mountain

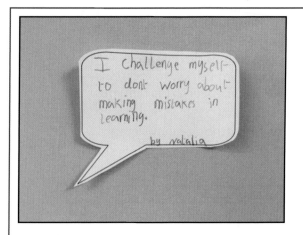
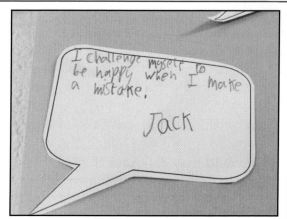
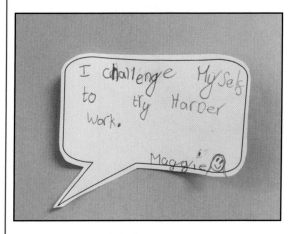

Figure 40 Personal challenges

An example of a child's alternative explanation of learning

'Learning in Colour Zones' by Alex age 7

❝In the red zone you are frustrated and not learning. The next zone is orange, where you might begin to learn but it's not your best. Next is blue where you are swimming in the learning sea, with your head above water. Finally, there is the green zone like a grassy field in summer where everyone is happy and you are trying your best. There is a lot of learning and you are challenging yourself.❞

Downloadable resources

PowerPoint presentation: picture of a giant mountain
bit.ly/2dZIGtX

6 Ding ding! How much effort?

Learning objectives	Resources
• To identify the different stages of effort • To create their own effort meter	• Learning behaviours vocabulary cards (Figure 41) • Effort meter template (Figure 42) • Giant effort meter (like, for example, Figure 43)

Lesson

1 *Ensure the children are sitting with their talk partner.*

Give each pair a set of the vocabulary cards of different learning behaviours (Figure 41).

Look at the behaviours and read them with the children and then ask them to read them back to you.

Ask the children to work with a talk partner to sort the cards into groups. Again, explain that there are no right or wrong answers. Once the discussions are underway, you should undertake the role of a learning facilitator. Listen to what the children are saying as it will reveal a lot about their attitudes to learning and their individual mindsets. Try not to intervene since allowing pupils to resolve issues with their talk partner is an important skill for them to develop. Again, you might wish to make a note of the children's responses to allow you to revisit misconceptions at a later point or share ideas through a display.

concentrating	challenging yourself	misbehaving	improving
giving up	responding to a challenge set by a teacher	persevering	practising

Figure 41 Learning behaviours vocabulary cards

2 Once the discussions are underway, you need to choose the right moment to intervene with an extension activity. This is always tricky, as you do not want to interrupt the children's discussion but you need to ensure the learning continues to develop. Ask them to discuss:

Are there any other behaviours which could be added to your different groups?

Randomly select pairs of children to share their ideas.

Giant effort!

3   Show the children a giant blank effort meter that is divided into four colours (Figure 43 shows an example of a completed effort meter). Ask the children to match the different behaviours to the four different stages of effort. Again, extend the discussions further by asking the children:

Are there any other behaviours which could be added to your different groups?

Bringing it together – what have we learned?

Children create their own individual effort meter using the template shown in Figure 42. They can then use this to reflect on their learning. They should personalise it and include their own learning behaviours for each stage.

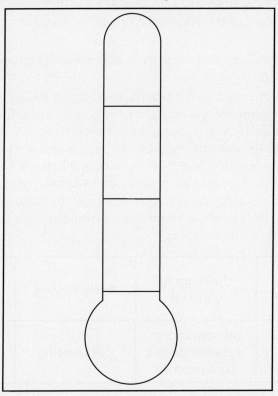

Figure 42 Template for an individual effort meter

Challenge

Ask the children to debate whether they always put the same amount of effort into their learning.

Further developments

Use the children's ideas to create a large effort meter for display. This can act as a visual prompt for learners and both children and teachers could give feedback for the learning in the classroom.

During learning, ask the children to reflect on their effort and use their individual effort meters to share their perceptions.

As the children's learning develops, you could revisit the effort meter and add additional characteristics.

Downloadable resources

Learning behaviours vocabulary cards

Template for an individual effort meter

bit.ly/2dLMWg8

Children's responses

Figure 43 Completed individual effort meter

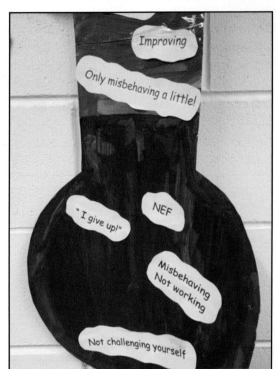

Figure 44 Close-up of individual effort meter

Lessons for 7–8 year olds
(Year 3, UK)

Lesson		Focus	Page
1	On the high wire	How someone feels when he or she fails; ways of encouraging someone to try	108
2	Firing neurons	What happens in your brain when you are learning something; what they think happens inside the brain of a growth/fixed mindset	111
3	Born to be …	The characteristics of growth and fixed mindsets; debating whether we are born to be good at something	114
4	Mistakes that worked	The importance of making mistakes as part of the learning process; creating a learning cycle to illustrate how something was created	122
5	Challenge mountains	Challenging areas and barriers to learning; developing ways to overcome these	127
6	Never give up!	How to overcome failure in different contexts; how it feels when we fail or make mistakes; creating a game that represents the process of learning	129

Overview

These lessons build on the previous learning about mistakes and overcoming failure. These themes are explored through a story and computer games. The idea is introduced that positive things can happen from mistakes. The brain and how it works is explored further and children are asked to begin to make links between the different mindsets and their own brain. Personal challenges are also revisited and reflected on in greater detail and these can be used to create a working display in the classroom.

1 On the high wire

Learning objectives	Resources
• To identify how someone feels when he or she fails • To suggest ways of encouraging someone to try	• Role badges (optional) • *Mirette on the High Wire* by Emily Arnold McCully • Visualiser or document camera (optional) • Flipchart showing images from the story and discussion points (see below)

Lesson

1 *During this lesson, the children will need to sit with their talk partner initially and then, as the lesson progresses, they will be sitting in learning groups at tables. You need to ensure your room is set up to encourage effective discussion between the children, such as square tables with four children sitting in twos facing each other. The tables could be arranged at a slight angle to ensure everyone can clearly see the board.*

Prior to beginning the lesson you might need to recap or introduce the different roles in the learning groups. This could be done using cards or posters as shown in Figure 25 on page 80. Explain to the children that they are going to work in learning groups with a specific role: **manager**, **reporter**, **encourager**, **recorder**. Role badges can be worn if desired.

You could have previously allowed the children to explore these roles when completing a simple task. This would allow them to become familiar with what their job entails. Initially it is advisable to allocate a specific role to a child and provide them with a number of opportunities to explore the same role. As the children become familiar and older, the roles can be changed regularly.

2 Show children the front cover of the story *Mirette on the High Wire*. Then ask them to discuss with their talk partner what they think the story might be about.

3 Read the story until the point where Mirette tries to walk on the wire and falls on to the ground on **page 9**. You could use a visualiser to share the book with the children. You could also zoom in on Mirette falling from the wire.

Ask the children to briefly discuss with their talk partner:

How does Mirette feel when she falls from the wire?

Look at the picture. How do you know she feels like that?

What would you do if you had tried to do something challenging like Mirette and couldn't do it?

What type of mindset is she demonstrating? How do you know?

During the discussions, you should use the strategy of 'eavesdropping'. This is where you listen to the discussions and make a note of the children's ideas. Then, rather than taking individual feedback, you share the ideas you gleaned from the discussions with the class.

On the high wire

4 *Ask the children to move into their learning groups.*

Then continue reading the book until Bellini admits to being afraid of failure and falling off the wire on **page 18**.

In their learning groups, ask the children to discuss:

How is Bellini feeling?

Why does he feel like that?

If you were Mirette, what would you say to Bellini?

Display the discussion points on cards or on the board so that the 'manager' can use them as a guide for the group discussions. Structure the discussion by slowly revealing each question to move the discussion on. During the discussions, you should undertake the role of a learning facilitator. Listen to what the children are saying as it will reveal a lot about their attitudes to learning and their individual mindsets. Try not to intervene since allowing pupils to resolve issues within their group is an important skill for them to develop. This allows them to develop as independent learners. You could make notes of the children's responses to allow you to revisit misconceptions at a later point or share ideas through a display.

5 Give the children a warning five minutes before asking them to feed back. This allows them to work together to ensure the reporter is fully prepared to feed back. If you feel it is appropriate, you could recap on what successful reporting looks like. The reinforcement of the success criteria will encourage children to develop their role of the reporter to a higher standard.

Initially, it might be useful to select a more confident or well-prepared child to deliver their group's feedback. Focus particularly on their ideas about what they could say to Bellini. Once the reporter has fed back, allow other members of the group to add to the discussions.

Bringing it together – what have we learned?

Extend the discussion further by asking the children to relate the character's experience to their own, using the next set of discussion points. Again, you could have the discussion points on cards or displayed on the board so that the manager can use them as a guide to the group discussions.

Is it easy to try again after failing?

What have you failed at? Did you try again?

What helped you to improve?

What strategies can you use to overcome your fear of failure?

Give the children five minutes of talk time to discuss their perceptions of failure before asking for feedback. You could select one question as a focus for the discussion.

During the discussions, you should continue to undertake the role of a learning facilitator, listening to the children rather than intervening as it will reveal a lot about their attitudes to learning and their individual mindsets. Again, you might wish to make a note of the children's responses to allow you to revisit misconceptions at a later point or share ideas through a display.

You could select groups randomly to feed back rather than asking every group, to ensure that the children remain focused and the lesson continues to develop at pace.

Challenge

Finish reading the story and then ask the children to discuss:

What helped Bellini to overcome his fear of making a mistake and failing?

Now ask the children to find other stories that contain characters who overcome barriers or challenges when learning to do something. A selection of these books could be displayed in class.

Further developments

Use the idea of the high wire for a display about learning and mindset. Photographs of the children could be displayed on the 'learning tightrope'. Incorporate examples of challenging learning on the high wire and ways of learning that help us to make progress such as practice or help from someone.

An alternative way of using the 'high wire of learning' would allow children to hang aspects of learning on it that they perceive to be challenging. Individual children could then remove them as they master the challenge or add another aspect to the wire. This can be very illuminating and reveal a lot about the children's perceptions.

In addition to the above activities, the children could write their own story about a character making a mistake and learning from it.

Children's responses

How would you encourage Bellini to try again?

‘When you have a fixed mindset your brain doesn't get bigger, it just locks. It locks down and just shuts down.’

‘I would take all of the people that said he was fantastic to speak to him and they would make him feel better about himself.’

‘Why are you worried to do it again when you have done it before?’

‘Tell him, that when he was a child he kept falling until he was a grown up.’

‘We decided that Bellini had a fixed mindset because he was terrified of going on the high wire again. Because of his fixed mindset he didn't dare go on the dangerous high wires again. We decided that if we were Mirette we would encourage Bellini to try to do the high wire and not be afraid.’

2 Firing neurons

Learning objectives	Resources
• To identify what happens in your brain when you are learning something • To describe what they think happens inside the brain of a growth/fixed mindset	• YouTube clip of firing neurons and brain at youtube.com/watch?v=TSwQOf4V3fE • The scene about what happens in the brain when you learn from the TV series *The Human Mind* • The video about how the brain works at cassiopeiaproject.com/videos2.php • Visualiser, document camera or tablet

Lesson

1 *Ensure the children have a clear view of the board and are sitting with their talk partner. This lesson begins with the video clip being used as a hook to focus the children's learning. This then leads to a focused discussion.*

Inform the children that they are going to watch a video clip and that they need to focus and ensure they watch it carefully. Watch the YouTube clip of neurons firing (without the sound). Perhaps watch it again to allow the children the chance to observe closely. There are many other examples on the internet which could be used to extend the discussion further.

Ask the children to discuss with their talk partner:

What do you think is happening in the clip? Why?

What is this film of?

When the discussions are underway and you feel it is appropriate you can develop them further by asking:

Can you suggest any words to describe what you saw?

How could you describe the movement?

Following some talk time, ask the children to feed back ideas to the class. You could pre-empt some children that they are going to share their ideas and then select children randomly to feed back. A useful strategy is the use of raffle tickets, with each child having a ticket and the teacher selecting a number of a child to feed back. Another method is to give every child a number and select the numbers using a bingo machine.

Learning and the mindset

2   Now watch the scene from the TV series *The Human Mind* that illustrates what is happening in the brain during learning. It uses the idea of learning creating bridges as connections are built in the brain. (If you cannot locate *The Human Mind*, describe the same idea to the children yourself.)

Ask the children to discuss:

What do you think the brain of someone with a growth mindset looks like?

What would you see happening in there?

Eavesdrop on the children's conversations and, when you feel it is the appropriate time, bring the children back together and again select children randomly to share their ideas.

3   Give the children some time to talk about:

What does the brain of someone with a fixed mindset looks like?

What would you see happening in there?

Do they work in the same way? Why?

Ask the children to feed back on their ideas and probe them further by asking them to explain why they think that.

4   Provide the children with plain paper and ask them to record what a brain with a growth mindset looks like and what a brain with a fixed mindset looks like.

Challenge the children further by asking them to label their pictures with explanations about what is happening.

Bringing it together – what have we learned?

Allow the children time to prepare to feed back their ideas. Pre-empt by saying that you would like them to explain as follows:

What do you think brains working with the different mindsets look like?

How do you think they work? Why?

Use a visualiser or tablet to share their recordings.

Explain that scientists have identified how a fixed mindset and a growth mindset can cause the brain to work in different ways. For further information on this, see 'Introduction by Shirley Clarke' (page 1).

Challenge

You could develop this further by watching the video at cassiopeiaproject.com/videos2.php giving a more complex explanation of how the brain works.

Further developments

When teaching and setting challenging tasks, explain to the children that you have set the task to make their neurons fire. Reinforce the language while teaching.

When discussing learning in lessons and giving feedback, ask:

Whose neurons are firing when they are learning something new?

Children's responses

Following the video clip showing neurons firing, what do you think is happening?

'It's your brain working, the lights are on and moving.'

'The lights are your brain being unlocked.'

What words would you use to describe what you have seen?

'Faster and faster as new ideas are formed.'

'Messy'

'Super signals'

'Slimy-alien like'

'Creating things inside it.'

What do you think happens in a brain with a growth mindset?

'It keeps on learning new things.'

'Inside your brain connections are growing.'

'It's faster at learning, it has strong pathways.'

'It gets heavier as you have more knowledge.'

'It is green and black in colour.'

'The colour of the brain changes as connections develop.'

What does a fixed mindset look like?

'It's red and black like a volcano, ideas are being drawn out as you are not listening and you have a fixed mindset.'

'It has more gaps as they give up so they haven't learnt enough to build a bridge across the gaps.'

'Like a volcano when it erupts (when someone gives up) or thinks they are clever.'

3 Born to be …

Learning objectives	Resources
• To identify the characteristics of growth and fixed mindsets • To debate whether we are born to be good at something	• Group role badges (optional) • Pictures of Usain Bolt or a similar athlete/sportsperson • Information about Usain Bolt (Figure 45) or another athlete

Lesson

1 *During this lesson, the children will need to sit with their talk partner initially and then, as the lesson progresses, the children will be sitting in learning groups at tables. You need to ensure your room is set up to encourage effective discussion between the children, such as square tables with four children sitting in twos facing each other. The tables could be arranged at a slight angle to ensure everyone can clearly see the board.*

Prior to beginning the lesson, you could have recapped on the different roles in the learning groups. This could be done using cards or posters as in Figure 25 on page 80 and asking the children to briefly discuss what makes an effective manager. This can be repeated for the different roles, or each learning group could discuss how to be effective at a specific role. The children's ideas could then be added to the posters to improve them and to give the children ownership of them.

Explain to the children that they are going to work in learning groups with a specific role: **manager**, **reporter**, **encourager** and **recorder**. You might want to use role badges.

You might have previously allowed the children to explore these roles when completing a simple task. This would allow them to become familiar with what their job entails. Initially it is advisable to allocate a specific role to a child and to provide them with a number of opportunities to explore the same role. As the children become familiar with the idea and more mature the roles can be changed regularly.

2 Reveal the word '**debate**' on the board. Ask the children to discuss as a learning group what they think this word means and how you should behave when debating.

While the discussions are taking place, observe the children and, when you think it is an appropriate moment, bring the discussions to a close and ask the groups for feedback. Through careful questioning, reach an agreement on a shared definition of 'debate'. Examples of possible questions to develop this are:

Do you agree a debate is where we …?

What should you do if you disagree with someone's ideas?

Do we have to agree with everyone's ideas?

Will there be a right or wrong answer?

This could be developed further by creating a brief list of behaviours we should see when a debate is happening, for example, sharing ideas or listening and responding to people's suggestions.

Born to be …

3 Show the children the pictures of Usain Bolt. Ask the following questions to elicit their prior knowledge:

Who is this?

What do you know about him?

Develop this further by providing background information about his achievements (see Figure 45). There is also a useful page about his achievements at www.biography.com.

Usain Bolt

He trains for 90 minutes at least 4 times a day.

Even though he loves chicken nuggets, he tries to go for 3 months without them.

Instead, on a typical day, he eats:

Did you know …?

Breakfast: Ackee and saltfish (a traditional Jamaican dish) with dumplings, cooked banana, yellow yam and potato

Lunch: Pasta and chicken breast

Dinner: Rice and peas with pork

Figure 45 Facts about Usain Bolt

4 Then pose the question:

Was Usain Bolt born to be a runner?

In their learning groups, ask the children to debate:

Do you think that you can be born to be good at something? Why?

How did Usain Bolt become an athlete and win medals for running? What has helped him to improve?

Have the discussion points on cards or displayed on the board so that the 'manager' can use them as a guide to the group discussions. Structure the discussion by slowly revealing each question to move the discussion on. You could also provide paper for the children to record their ideas on, perhaps in a simple 'agree and disagree' format or using the worksheet (see Figure 46).

During the discussions, you should undertake the role of a learning facilitator. Listen to what the children are saying as it will reveal a lot about their attitudes to learning and their individual mindsets. Try not to intervene since allowing pupils to resolve issues within their group is an important skill for them to develop. This allows them to develop as independent learners. You could make a note of the children's responses to allow you to revisit misconceptions at a later point or share ideas through a display.

Give the children a warning five minutes before asking them to feed back. This allows them to work together to ensure the reporter is fully prepared to feed back. If you feel it is appropriate, you could recap what successful reporting looks like. The reinforcement of the success criteria will encourage the children to develop their role of the reporter to a higher standard.

Was Usain Bolt born to be …?

Yes, he was because …	No, he wasn't because ….

Figure 46 Worksheet for 'born to be…?'

Bringing it together – what have we learned?

Ask the groups to feed back on their debates and to share key discussion points. Once the reporter has finished feedback, you may wish to allow other members of the group to add to the feedback.

To probe the feedback further, you could ask the following questions:

Would you have a different opinion if you were debating whether a person were born to be an artist or a footballer and so on?

Do you think that you are born to be good at something?

Did everyone in the group agree?

Challenge

Ask the children to suggest people to be debated as whether they are born to be … Short films can be made showing both sides of the debate. This can also be included in a display through the use of QR codes.

Further developments

This activity can be adapted in a range of ways. You can select a different famous person to capture the children's interest and provoke discussion. The world of sport provides a range of contexts, as does the news, films and music.

A display could be created that incorporates a range of people and shows the learning journey they went on to achieve success. Children's comments taken from the debate could be included as talking points.

Downloadable resources

PowerPoint presentation about Usain Bolt
Worksheet 'Was Usain Bolt born to be …?'

bit.ly/2dmvmPk

Children's responses

What does the word 'debate' mean?

> *A big conversation.*

> *It's where one person wants one thing and another person wants something else.*

> *It's virtually an argument but you don't fall out.*

> *It's like an argument where people think of different reasons to disagree with opinions.*

Guidance for debates

> *Make sure everyone gets the opportunity to speak.*

> *Don't interrupt!*

> *Be kind.*

> *Listen to each other.*

> *Look at whoever is speaking.*

> *Don't go over the top or be cross when you're arguing.*

> *Be friendly and sensible.*

> *Make sure you give reasons for your opinions.*

> *You can always say we'll agree to disagree.*

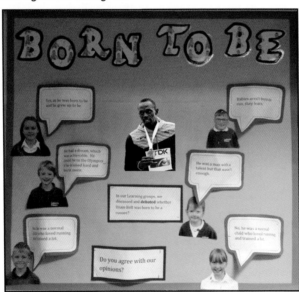

Figure 47 Born to be …

Was Usain Bolt born to be an athlete?

> *No, he was a normal child who loved running and trained a lot.*

> *Babies aren't born to run, they learn.*

> *He had a dream, which was achievable. He could be in the Olympics if he trained hard and learnt more.*

'Yes, as he was born to be and he grew up to be.'

'He was a man with a talent but that wasn't enough.'

'He could have been born to be something else!'

Was Usain Bolt born to be......?

our group decided that...

Yes, he was because...	No, he wasn't because....
"that is what he grew up to be. ·his dad might have been an athlete so he decided to become one.	·He decided to become an athlete. ·He had to train to become an athlete ·He wasn't famous when he was a baby. ~~yes he was born to be fa~~ ·He wasn't born an athlete

Was Usain Bolt born to be......?

Yes, he was because...	No, he wasn't because....
	he just tried as hard as he could & never gave up, he even tried not to eat one of his favourite foods! We also think that he wasn't born to be he just had the idea in his head & tried to make it happen.

~~he was~~ born to be a runner and was

🏃Was Usain Bolt born to be......?

4 ?.

Yes, he was because...	No, he wasn't because....
yes because he was the fastest sprinter. yes because he exersized everey day yes because he is a good runner. yes because he has won so many medals yes he is a good runner because he eat healthy food.	No because not many peopel are ~~not~~ ment to be the fastod runner in the world. No because he Traind to be an afaleed he could of bin played Foot ball.

Figure 48 Was Usain Bolt born to be …?

Was David Beckham born to be a talented footballer?

ceeps on practising

He lissens to his coach.
He pratsis evry day.
David traind and traind unti
good foot ball player.
He made good porgres.
He leant diffrant skils.
He was so good he

Figure 49 Was David Beckham born to be …?

4 Mistakes that worked

Learning objectives	Resources
• To identify the importance of making mistakes as part of the learning process • To create a learning cycle to illustrate how something was created	• Images of items invented by mistake (see Figure 50) • *Mistakes that Worked* by Charlotte Foltz Jones • The invention of the frisbee (Figure 51) • Visualiser or document camera • Article 'Inventions that were mistakes' at mag.amazing-kids.org

Lesson

1 *Arrange the children so they are sitting with their talk partner and can see the board.*

Have ready some images of objects that were created by mistake (see Figure 50). You will find a range of examples in the book *Mistakes that Worked*. Try to personalise it by including examples that would be of interest to your children, for example, coca cola, the slinky, a frisbee, the piggy bank and sticky notes.

Slowly reveal the images and ask the children:

What can you see?

2 Invite the children to discuss what they think all the different items have in common:

Can you think of a reason why these items are connected?

Ask them to think of as many possible connections as they can. Following some talk time, ask the children to feed back ideas to the class. You could pre-empt some children that they are going to share their ideas and then select children randomly to feed back, perhaps by using lollipop sticks.

Once you have taken feedback from the children, reveal to them that all of the items were actually created by mistake. The inventors had not planned to create them – they were made by accident!

Connections

Can you think of a reason why these items are connected?

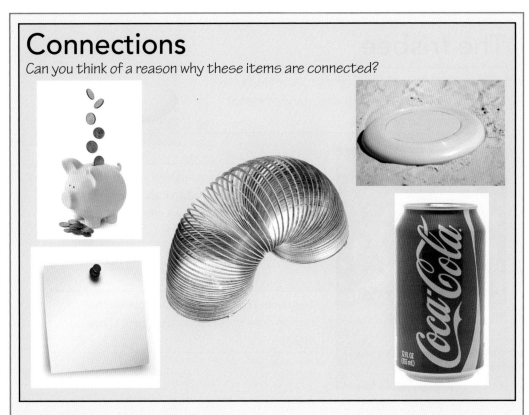

Figure 50 Connections – mistakes that worked

The frisbee mistake

3 Explain that you are going to share the story of how the frisbee was invented. Read the story taken from the book *Mistakes that Worked.* You could also display some key points about how it was invented on the board (see Figure 51).

Re-read the story and then ask the children to think about the key points in the frisbee's creation. Provide the children with talk time to discuss this. Structure the discussions by asking the children to think about the following points, gradually revealing each point, taking feedback and then moving on:

What was the original idea?

What things caused the creation of the frisbee?

Can you describe the frisbee now?

How would you present this?

The frisbee

The original frisbee was a pie tin stamped with the words 'Frisbie Pies'. It was made of metal. It was made to hold pies.

It would have done nothing except hold pies if some students at Yale hadn't decided to eat the pies and then play a game by tossing the tins to each other.

They would call 'frisbie' as they threw the tins to warn people that they were throwing objects.

Figure 51 How the frisbee was invented

4 When appropriate, develop this theme further by asking the children to create a learning cycle to represent how the frisbee was created by mistake. Allow the children access to a range of resources such as different pens and paper of various sizes.

To support this activity, perhaps model possible ways of presenting the journey of a frisbee and how it was invented, for example, as a cycle.

Using a visualiser, share some of the examples of the frisbee's learning journey and review how the children have represented them.

Bringing it together – what have we learned?

Ask the children to think about their own learning journey and when they make mistakes. Ask them to talk to their talk partner about:

When do you make mistakes?

What happens when you make a mistake?

How do you feel when you make a mistake?

What happens when you learn?

How do mistakes help?

Once again, take feedback from the children and probe their ideas further:

Why do you think that?

Can you explain why you feel like that?

Challenge

Provide the children with their exercise books. Ask them to identify key mistakes they have made and reflect:

Why do you think you made those mistakes?

What did you learn from them?

What would you do differently if you could go back?

How could you get better at this?

What do you do now if you are stuck in your learning?

Further developments

The children could choose one of the items displayed at the beginning of the lesson and write a report on how it was created by mistake. They could use their imagination to create a plausible explanation.

Other examples of items created by mistake are discussed in the article 'Inventions that were mistakes' at mag.amazing-kids.org.

Downloadable resources

PowerPoint presentation about items invented by mistake

PowerPoint presentation about how the frisbee was invented

Video of children discussing mistakes

bit.ly/2e3BxWI

Children's responses

What things caused the creation of the frisbee?

> 'It wasn't made to be a toy, it happened by accident as they were playing a game.'

> 'The shape helped.'

> 'It was a mistake, it wasn't meant to be a game.'

> 'People used it differently.'

How do you feel when you make mistakes?

> 'I know mistakes are part of the learning process.'

> 'When you make mistakes, the next time you make the same mistake again, you can correct them.'

> 'Don't shout at people who make mistakes in learning as they are learning from it.'

> 'If you were starting to learn long division, at first you may make lots of mistakes. Don't give up! You are learning from it.'

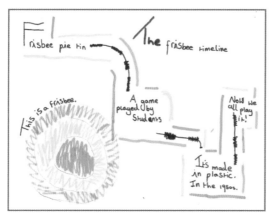

Figure 52 The frisbee timeline

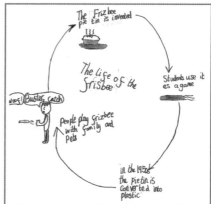

Figure 53 The life of the frisbee

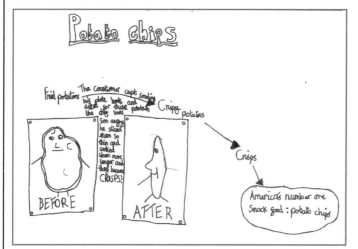

Figure 54 Inventing the crisp

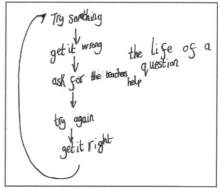

Figure 55 The life of a question

5 Challenge mountains

Learning objectives	Resources
• To identify an area that you find challenging and the barriers to learning • To develop ways of overcoming barriers to learning	• Challenge mountain vocabulary cards (Figure 56) • Visualiser or document camera • Materials to build challenge mountains

Lesson

1 *Seat children with their talk partners.*

   Introduce the key vocabulary to the children and invite them to sort the words into groups. Ask them to discuss what the words mean and why they have grouped them together.

   After talk time, ask children to feed back their ideas.

effort	challenge	personal
mistake	overcome	determined
error	motivation	difficult

Figure 56 Challenge mountain vocabulary cards

2 Model an aspect of learning that you have found difficult. Explain to the children the barriers to your learning. Ask the children to discuss with their talk partner how they would help you to overcome the barriers. Using a visualiser, model what your challenge mountain would look like and how you would illustrate the barriers.

Climbing your mountain

3 Ask the children to discuss:

   What have you found challenging?

   What barriers are there?

   How could you overcome the barriers?

4 Then provide the children with materials to create their own challenge mountains.

Bringing it together – what have we learned?

Children share their challenge mountains using the visualiser. Ask them to describe their mountain and the barriers to their learning and how they would overcome them.

Display the children's mountains in the classroom as a visual reminder of their learning journey and how they are trying to improve.

Challenge

Ask the children to suggest an alternative image that they could use to illustrate a learning challenge. They could write a guide for a younger child, using an image to reinforce the idea, explaining what happens when we are learning. Encourage the children to focus on the ideas and the explanation and not to make the image too elaborate so that it takes up most of their time.

Further developments

Children should be encouraged to move themselves independently on the challenge mountain to reflect the progress they are making on their learning journey.

Once children have been successful with their learning challenge, the mountains can be adapted for a new challenge.

Downloadable resources

Challenge mountain vocabulary cards
bit.ly/2dLOjLJ

Children's responses

Figure 57 Moving up my challenge mountain

Figure 58 You can do this!

6 Never give up!

Learning objectives	Resources
• To discuss how we overcome failure in different contexts • To describe how it feels when we fail or make mistakes • To create a game that represents the process of learning	• Images of computer games and children learning in school • A YouTube clip of a challenging scenario in Minecraft • Visualiser or document camera (optional) • Materials to design a game

Lesson

1 *Arrange the children so they are sitting with their talk partner and can clearly see the board.*

Show the children some images of a range of computer games, for example 'Minecraft', 'SIMs', 'Terraria' and 'Lego Star Wars', and an image of children learning in school. Ask them initially to think about which is the odd one out and why? Next they should discuss their ideas with a talk partner. Take feedback from the children about their ideas.

2 Ask the children to put up their hands if they play computer games.

Develop the discussion further by asking the children to think about and then discuss with their talk partner:

How do you feel when you fail or make a mistake with your learning?

How do you feel when you fail or make a mistake when playing a computer game?

When you are playing a computer game, do you give up and never play again?

Do you feel differently when you make a mistake when playing a game or when you are learning in school?

3 Show the children a YouTube clip of a challenging scenario in Minecraft. Then, presenting one question at a time, ask the children to discuss and reflect on:

How would you feel if you were playing this game?

Would you give up? Why/why not?

Do we behave in the same way when we are playing challenging games as we do when we are learning?

Learning games

4 Explain to the children that they are all game designers/programmers and that they have been asked to create a learning game where the process of learning is made into a computer game.

Ask the children to think about:

What does a successful game have?

What would your learning game look like?

What could make your characters fail or challenge them?

How would you be successful?

5 Provide the children with paper and a range of materials to design their game.

Bringing it together – what have we learned?

Once they have completed their designs, randomly select a few children to share and explain their ideas – perhaps using a visualiser. Allow the children time to reflect on each other's ideas and to ask questions.

Challenge

Ask the children to create a list of similarities and differences for how they feel when they make a mistake when playing a computer game compared to when they are learning in school.

Further developments

Have a class debate with the children working in their learning groups:

Do children give up more when learning in school than when playing computer games?

Children can use simple coding to create a learning game using images.

Downloadable resources

PowerPoint presentation 'Which is the odd one out?'
bit.ly/2dLOjLJ

Lessons for 8–9 year olds (Year 4, UK)

Lesson		Focus	Page
1	From failure to success	Valuing failure as an important part of the learning process; defining the term 'successful'	132
2	Bounce!	Strategies for persevering and learning when they make a mistake; describing how they feel when they make a mistake	136
3	Doom words	Words that can restrict us as learners; creating our own words to describe the learning process	141
4	Mindset trumps	Characteristics of an effective learner; suggesting justification for awards; creating a simple game	144
5	Fantastic elastic brain	Identifying the characteristics of growth and fixed mindsets; debating whether we are born to be good at something	149
6	Learning cereals	Characteristics of an effective learner; creating a design for a learning cereal packaging	155

Overview

These lessons are designed to deepen the children's understanding of the brain and how it works when we learn. The idea of personalised learning is reinforced. Failure and its role in the learning process is developed further as the children reflect on failures who became famous and what factors enabled them to achieve. Key vocabulary is revisited and defined, including the effective characteristics of a learner. Children are also encouraged to reflect on language that might have a negative impact on learning and how they can develop a more positive approach through the language they use.

1 From failure to success

Learning objectives	Resources
• To identify and value how failure is an important part of the learning process • To define the term 'successful'	• Photographs of famous people (see Figure 60) • Background information about these people (see Figure 60) • Additional information (see Figure 60)

Lesson

1 *Arrange the children so they are sitting with their talk partner and are able to see the board clearly.*

   Share with the children the four photographs and the background information about these famous people (see Figure 60, but use different famous people if they are more appropriate for your children):

   • Jo Pavey   • Walt Disney
   • J.K. Rowling   • Bill Gates

   Read the background information on each person together. You could build some talk time in here to allow the children to discuss any words that are unfamiliar such as 'entrepreneur'.

2 Then ask the children to work with their partner to put the photographs in order according to which person they think is the most successful. Remind the children that there is no right or wrong answer and that you are just interested in their opinion.

   Once they have completed the activity, ask the children for feedback:

   Who was the most successful?

   Why do you think that?

   Who was the least successful? Why?

   Were you and your partner in agreement?

3 With their talk partner, ask the children to discuss:

   What does the word 'successful' mean?

   Then take feedback from them and challenge the children's thinking by asking:

   Does it always mean that you're the best?

   Would that make you change your order? Why?

   If it means … how would this affect your ordering?

   Give the children time to revisit their ordering.

Famous failures

4 Provide the children with the additional information on how the famous people failed (see Figure 60), read it together and then allow the talk partners to re-visit their ordering.

Ask the children:

Does the additional information make you change your ordering? If so, why?

Use lollipop sticks to randomly select children to answer the questions, thus ensuring all children are focused. Remember to pre-empt them prior to the start of the discussion that you will be doing this.

Famous people			

Background information			
Jo Pavey won a gold medal at the age of 40 in 2014 in the 10,000 m. She is the oldest female European champion in history.	Walt Disney is the creator of Mickey Mouse and the winner of 22 Academy Awards.	J.K. Rowling wrote the Harry Potter books and has sold more than 400 million books around the world. They have become the bestselling books in the world.	Bill Gates is the co-founder of Microsoft. He is one of the best known entrepreneurs in the world. He is worth an estimated US$81.8 billion.
Additional information			
In the 2002 Commonwealth games Jo Pavey came 5th and in the 2012 European Championships she came 7th.	Walt Disney was fired from a newspaper and told that 'he lacked imagination and had no good ideas'.	J.K. Rowling sent her book to 12 publishers and it was rejected by them all. When it was finally accepted she was told not to give up her job as the book probably would not sell.	While studying at university, he failed his exams. The first business Bill Gates started was a complete failure.

Figure 60 Famous people – pictures, background information, additional information

Bringing it together – what have we learned?

You should then provide some personal information about something you have failed at, for example, Mrs Muncaster failed her driving test twice but she had extra lessons and practice to help and then finally passed it on the third attempt. It is important to model failure to the children so they see it as part of everyday life.

Ask the children to discuss:

How do you feel when you fail?

Can you give an example of something you've failed at?

What could you do differently?

How do you overcome failure?

How did your failure help you learn?

The teacher should work in role as a facilitator while the children discuss this. Listen to what the children are saying as it will reveal a lot about their attitudes to learning and their individual mindsets. Try not to intervene since allowing pupils to resolve issues with their partner is an important skill for them to develop.

Then choose some children to feed back their discussions. Be sensitive and discuss beforehand with the child whether he or she is happy to share.

Challenge

Ask the children to debate:

When do you think you learn more – when you succeed or when you fail?

Further developments

In an extended write, the children should write a report on failure and include some of the information from the session, alongside further research and a personal reflection on failure.

Downloadable resources

PowerPoint presentation about famous people

bit.ly/2dmvm1W

Children's responses

Who was the most successful?

> 'J.K. Rowling, Jo Pavey, Bill Gates and then Walt Disney. We think J.K. Rowling is the most successful because of the number of books she has published. Jo Pavey is next because she won a medal. Bill Gates is next because he made the internet work. Walt Disney is not as important as he just made fun films.'

> 'Bill Gates, Walt Disney, J.K. Rowling, and then Jo Pavey. Bill Gates is on the internet and everyone uses Microsoft. He also earns a lot of money. Then Walt Disney as he makes amazing films. Then J.K. Rowling as people love her books and finally Jo Pavey as the others are more famous, we don't really know her.'

> 'Walt Disney, Bill Gates, J.K. Rowling and then Jo Pavey. Walt Disney is first because lots of people watch his films; they are all over the world. Bill Gates created lots of useful things by himself. Then it's J.K. Rowling as she wrote lots of books that people love. Last is Jo Pavey as she is really old and we haven't seen her on television.'

What does the word successful mean?

> 'It means you have achieved something.'

> 'You did it.'

> 'If you were playing football, you may have got too old but you could have been successful.'

> 'It means you got to the top.'

Did your ordering change? Why?

> 'We thought about the bad things that had happened and changed it. Bill Gates overcame the most so he is the most successful.'

> 'Bill Gates first and then Walt Disney next because Walt Disney did try very hard.'

> 'Walt Disney last because he was fired and was less successful.'

Another child responded to the above comment:

> 'But he didn't give up so he was successful.'

How do you feel when you fail?

> 'Unhappy.'

> 'You might feel like you want to try again, it is only your first attempt.'

> 'When you fail does it mean you are bad at something or a learner?'

> 'I really wanted to be in the football team but they kept not picking me so I kept practising and going to training. I kept trying and then I got picked.'

2 Bounce!

Learning objectives	Resources
• To identify strategies for persevering and learning when they make a mistake • To describe how they feel when they make a mistake	• Picture of a child frustrated by learning (Figure 61) • Large balls (one inflated and one not) • Bouncy balls • Permanent markers

Lesson

1 *Organise the classroom so that the children are sitting with their talk partner and can see the board.*

Show the children a picture of a child feeling frustrated in his or her learning. Ask them to discuss with their talk partner:

How is the child in the picture feeling?

How do you feel when you make a mistake?

Figure 61 A boy frustrated by learning

Explain to the children that there is no right or wrong answer to the second question and that you are just interested in their opinion. While the children discuss this, the teacher should eavesdrop: ideally there should be a mixture of feedback from those who become frustrated by their mistakes and those who see it as a part of the learning journey.

Take feedback from the children, using questioning to probe their perceptions. The strategy of posing a question, then pausing to allow thinking time and then finally pouncing would be extremely effective here. It would ensure the children had the opportunity to reflect and share their opinions while allowing the lesson to continue to develop.

How do you feel when you make a mistake? Why?

When do you feel like that?

Do you feel you make mistakes more often in a particular subject?

Do you deal with mistakes differently depending on the subject? Why do you think this is?

Why do you think we have different opinions?

Bounce

2 Show the children two balls, one inflated and one not. Ask the children to watch what happens when you (or two children) drop the different balls.

Again, ask the children to talk to their talk partner:

What happened when we dropped the inflated ball?

What happened to the deflated ball?

What do you think the two balls represent?

If necessary, explain to the children that the inflated ball has a growth mindset and that the deflated ball has a fixed mindset.

3 Ask the children to think about the different ways the mindsets cause you to respond to mistakes. The children should record the ways and characteristics on paper or on a bouncy/deflated ball.

You may wish to give the children an example of how the different mindsets can affect how we respond to mistakes. For example, if you have a fixed mindset you would give up but with a growth mindset you will challenge yourself and try to find a new strategy. A growth mindset bounces into learning.

To differentiate the activity, you could provide examples of responses for children to sort instead.

Bringing it together – what have we learned?

Ask the children to feed back and share examples of the different ways they can respond to mistakes. Emphasise the importance of having to BOUNCE BACK after a mistake as it is part of the learning process.

To encourage the children to think of a range of specific strategies, ask them to discuss:

Is it enough just to keep trying?

Is that all we need to do to get better?

Provide the children with some time to talk to their partner and then, when you feel it is an appropriate point in the discussions, ask them to feed back. Initially take feedback by asking the children to vote on whether they agree with the statements and then develop this further by asking them to explain their thinking.

To develop this discussion further you could model to the children trying to solve a calculation using the same strategy repeatedly. Then ask the children:

What can I do to improve?

Should I just keep trying the same method?

Responses you are hoping to encourage include:
- Doesn't give up
- Asks a partner for help
- Tries again
- Learns a new strategy
- Revisits their learning
- Receives intervention
- Asks a teacher to help
- Understands it's part of the learning process
- Practises and goes back to first steps

Challenge

Can you think of a different word or phrase to describe a mistake?

Do you think there is a specific order in which you should attempt the different strategies following a mistake?

Further developments

Create a display using the two balls and the different ways the children respond to mistakes. Add to the board as the children show different responses across the curriculum.

Children's responses

How do you feel when you make a mistake?

'Angry'

'Happy, as when you make a mistake you're learning. You don't need to worry, just try again.'

'Cross because you have to rub it out which makes your work a mess.'

'Happy as you can learn from your mistakes.'

'Upset but not too angry, maybe angry inside.'

'I make more mistakes in maths as I don't really get it.'

'In English there's no right answers, there can be lots of answers but in maths you need a right answer.'

'I act the same, as a mistake is a mistake whatever lesson. You just need to learn from it.'

'You get used to dealing with mistakes in subjects you find hard.'

'If you get more confident with something you worry less.'

'When you are little you can have a different attitude, in Year 1 you get very frustrated when you make a mistake but as you get older you can control it. As you get older you think more about your learning behaviour.'

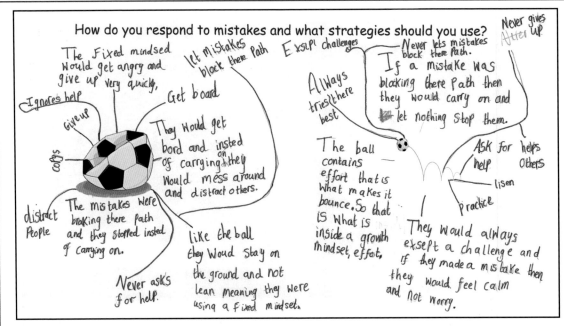

Figure 62 How to respond to mistakes (1)

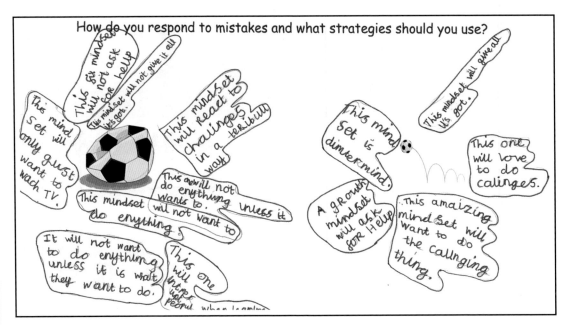

Figure 63 How to respond to mistakes (2)

Figure 64 Bounce poster

Downloadable resources

PowerPoint presentation of a child frustrated by learning
Video of children discussing mistakes

bit.ly/2e3Ccrb

3 Doom words

Learning objectives	Resources
• To identify words and phrases that can restrict us as learners • To create our own words to describe the learning process	• Doom words and learning words (Figure 65)

Lesson

1 *Arrange the children so they are sitting with their talk partner and can see the board.*

Show the children the word '**easy**' and ask them to discuss with their talk partner what they think it means. Explain you are interested in their opinions rather than there being a correct answer.

Once the discussions are underway, allow the children enough time to share their opinions and then, at the appropriate moment, bring the class back together. Take feedback from the children.

Develop this further by asking the children:

Do you like easy learning?

Allow them to respond using a show of hands and then probe their responses further by asking:

Why do you like/dislike easy learning?

Do you always like easy learning in every lesson?

2 Next pose the question:

Do you think that the word 'easy' is bad for learning?

Again, give the children some time to discuss this with their partner. During the discussions you should 'eavesdrop' on the conversations as this will allow you to observe the different opinions and misconceptions and to select children with opinions that differ to feed back.

If the children suggest that 'easy' could be both a useful word and a negative word, probe this further, as some children will identify that as they learn to do something it becomes easy.

Doom words

3 Explain that some words can be described as 'doom words'. These are words that can be bad for learning like 'easy'.

It would be useful at this point to provide an anecdote of someone's learning behaviour and you could personalise this to reflect the learning behaviour of the children you teach. For example: '**Fred likes to be** the first to finish and always says very loudly "finished!" Fred isn't concerned about challenging himself – instead he is more focused on being quicker than other children and finishing his learning first.'

4 Encourage the children to think about any other words or phrases that could be described as doom words. Ask them to discuss examples with their talk partner or to write a list.

If appropriate, you could differentiate the activity by providing the children with words to sort into doom words or learning words (Figure 65) before asking them to think of some of their own.

easy	learning	challenge
right	first to finish	determined
boring	mistake	difficult

Figure 65 Doom words and learning words

Bringing it together – what have we learned?

Ask the children to share their ideas with the class and then select some suggestions that can be turned into positive learning phrases and words, for example: 'I can't …' can become 'I can't YET!'

Ask the children to suggest ways of changing a doom phrase into a learning phrase. Initially, you might need to model different ways of doing this, for example: 'I can't do this … so please can you help me.'

Challenge

During the doom word discussion, the children could record their ideas in a Venn diagram to show words that can be learning words, doom words or both.

Further developments

You could extend the discussion by asking the children to discuss and identify 'doom' learning behaviours.

Ask the children to create a poster to promote the school/classroom as a learning zone where doom words are not acceptable.

Share the idea that, at some point, learning a particular skill should become easier. For example, they could not do column addition at first but, with lots of practice, they managed to master it and it became 'easy' because of their resilience and thirst for learning. Ask the children to reflect on their learning and share their own examples of having mastered a particular skill.

Downloadable resources

Doom word and learning word cards

bit.ly/2ejC8YP

Children's responses

What does 'easy' mean?

❛Easy means something you can do. It's the opposite of hard.❜

❛You can do it straight away, do it lots of times without getting it wrong.❜

❛It's simple.❜

❛You don't have to think about it like 2 + 2.❜

❛It's when something isn't challenging. But you must be careful about saying it to others as we all find different things easy and challenging.❜

Is the word easy bad for learning?

❛My opinion is that easy is bad for picking work as you need to challenge yourself.❜

❛It's both as when you have just started learning it could be hard but it should become easier.❜

❛Saying easy can upset and annoy others as they may find it hard.❜

❛It can have a negative impact as you need to challenge yourself in your learning and not choose easy!❜

What is a doom word?

❛Something that you shouldn't say.❜

❛We made doom words up as easy is a word that's bad for your learning.❜

❛You can have doom phrases like I give up.❜

❛We need bounce words that help you come back to learning.❜

4 Mindset trumps

Learning objectives	Resources
• To identify the characteristics of an effective learner • To suggest justification for why a character is awarded a given number of points for a characteristic • To create a simple game	• A mindset trumps card describing you, the teacher (see Figure 66) • Effective learner cards (Figure 67) • Mindset trumps template (Figure 68)/Top Trump It app • Visualiser or tablet

Lesson

1 *Ensure the children are sitting with their talk partner ready to talk and have a clear view of the board.*

Ask the children if they have ever played the Top Trumps® card game and to respond through a show of hands.

Ask them to discuss with their talk partner:

How do you play the game?

What makes you successful at it?

What can cause you to fail?

2 Show the children the mindset trumps card featuring yourself and look at the characteristics the points have been awarded for. Ask the children:

What have I been awarded points for?

What does … mean?

Figure 66 Teacher top trumps

Mindset trumps

3 Explain to the children that they are going to create their own mindset trumps using characters from children's books.

Explain that they should award points out of a hundred for each character. The points will be awarded for the characteristics of an effective learner. Ask the children to discuss with their talk partner:

What do you think makes an effective learner?

How should you behave when you are learning?

Take feedback from the children and review the suggestions. Ensure that all the children understand what the different words mean and, if appropriate, build in further talk time to allow the children to explore and clarify their understanding. Possible answers might include:

- effort
- resilience
- growth mindset
- desire to be challenged
- effective listener
- initiative
- honesty
- ability to ask for help.

If your pupils are unfamiliar with the characteristics of an effective learner, you could begin the lesson with this activity or you could provide them with the characteristics on cards (see Figure 67) along with other attributes that are not effective and ask children to sort them with a partner. Ensure you check that all of the children understand the vocabulary; use talk time and feedback to avoid misconceptions.

The following are examples of children's misconceptions and ways that they could be addressed by the teacher:

Possible misconception	Teacher's response
A child suggests making mistakes.	Would it be making mistakes or making mistakes and learning from them?
A child suggests kindness.	Does that make us an effective learner or a kind person?
A child suggests a negative characteristic.	Remodel it as a positive characteristic.

perseveres	likes to be challenged	likes to be right
likes easy work	first to finish	determined
worries about making a mistake	resilient	gives up

Figure 67 Characteristics of an effective learner vocabulary cards

4 The class should then decide which four different characteristics they are going to award points for.

Revisit your example of a mindset trumps card for yourself and model awarding yourself points for the four chosen characteristics. For example:

'I am going to award myself 50/100 points for resilience because I have a tendency to give up, particularly when writing and decorating. I need to try harder with this.'

'I am awarding myself 80/100 for resilience because I use mistakes as part of the learning process and don't get upset if I get something wrong.'

5   Explain that they are going to create a mindset trumps card for a given character and that they need to think carefully about the point allocation and provide reasons for this.

Perfect Peter, for example, would be awarded 20/100 for growth mindset because he always likes to be right. Ask the children to discuss with their talk partner possible reasons why Perfect Peter would only be awarded 20 points for the characteristic of having a growth mindset.

Allocate a character to each set of talk partners and either ask them to complete the template or use the Top Trump It app to create a card for a character. Try to include a range of characters that include a wide range of contexts where effective learning behaviours can be debated. Suggestions for characters include Horrid Henry, Perfect Peter and Charlie from *Charlie and the Chocolate Factory*.

It might be useful to have a word bank for some children to use, to remove any barriers to learning.

Provide copies of books or enable access to the internet so the children can research the characters. If you allow the children to choose their own character, you might wish to check that their characters are appropriate.

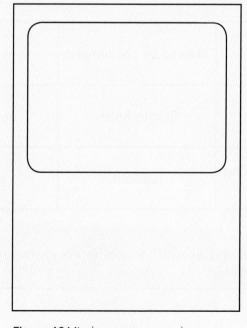

Figure 68 Mindset trumps template

Bringing it together – what have we learned?

Share the examples of the cards the children have created, ideally using a visualiser or by displaying the trump cards from the app.

Compare and contrast two cards and ask the children to justify why they have awarded the points for each characteristic. Then ask the class to debate if they agree how the points were awarded. Try to select two cards with glaring contrasts or an over-allocation of points in order to facilitate a deeper discussion.

This activity could be replicated by asking each set of talk partners to work with another pair to share their justification for the allocation of points.

Challenge

A variation on this game could be created using famous people (sporting personalities are extremely effective). The children could research their careers, identify the different characteristics and award points. Again, they would need to provide justification for the allocation of points.

Further developments

Children could create additional mindset trumps characters at home, which can be added to the class game.

You could create a display of the children in the class, asking them to identify which characteristics of an effective learner are their strengths and perhaps one aspect as an area for development. These can then be displayed and, as the area for development improves, the child or the class could award new points.

Downloadable resources

Characteristics of an effective learner vocabulary cards
Mindset trumps template
bit.ly/2dYR378

Children's responses

Perfect Peter	
Risilichs	4
groth minset	10
Lerning	20
Coneettason	99

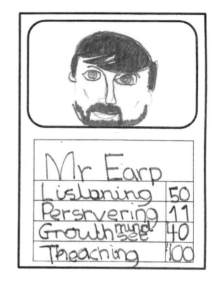

Mr Earp	
Lisloning	50
Persrvering	11
Growth minse see	40
Theaching	100

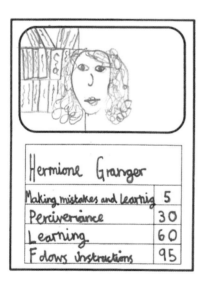

Hermione Granger	
Making mistakes and learning	5
Perciveriance	30
Learning	60
Folows instructions	95

Mr fox	
persiverance :	90
Lerning :	100
Resilance :	88
Essort :	100

Figure 69 Examples of children's mindset trumps

5 Fantastic elastic brain

Learning objectives	Resources
• To identify the characteristics of growth and fixed mindsets • To debate whether we are born to be good at something	• Odd one out examples (see Figure 70) • Elastic bands • *Your Fantastic Elastic Brain* by JoAnn M. Deak • Visualiser or document camera (optional)

Lesson

1 *Arrange the children so they are sitting with their talk partner and can see the board.*

Reveal the three images on Figure 70 to the children.

Explain that there are no right or wrong answers to the next question. Give the children time to discuss their ideas with their talk partner:

Which is the odd one out? Why?

Then develop their thinking further by asking them to think about:

Is there another odd one out?

Can you think of a different reason?

Take feedback from the children on their different ideas and reasons for something being the odd one out.

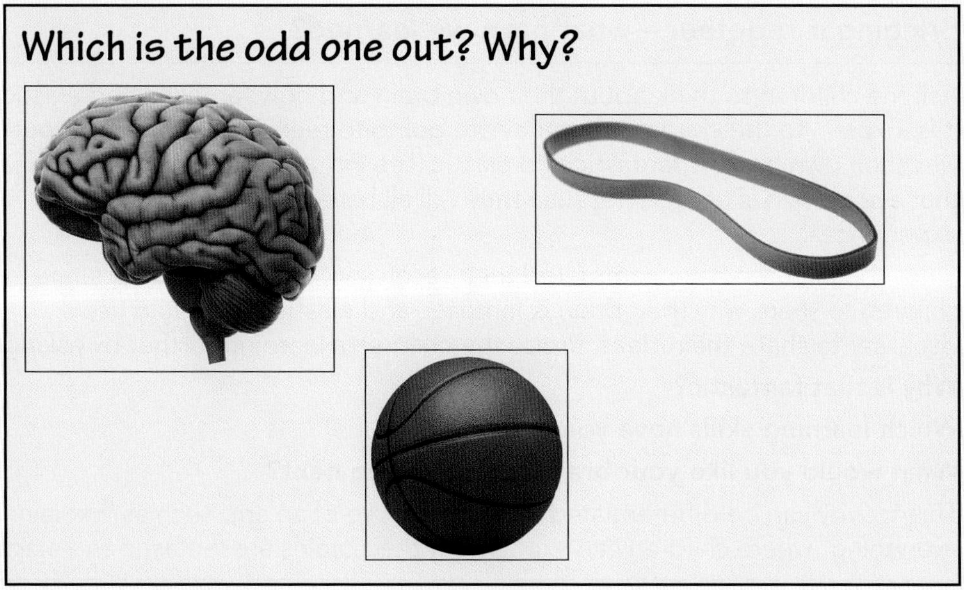

Which is the odd one out? Why?

Figure 70 Odd one out

Stretch and learn

2   Show the children an elastic band and model how it can be stretched and manipulated. Explain that you want them to think about why you have shown them an elastic band while they listen to you read the book.

3   Share the book *My Fantastic Elastic Brain* with the children. You could use a visualiser to share the book with the children. You could also use a flipchart to illustrate key examples of what the brain can do and how it works.

Next pose the following questions to encourage them to reflect on what they have heard:

Why do you think I showed you an elastic band at the start of the lesson?

What type of mindset enables your brain to be like an elastic band?

What did you learn from the book?

4   Explain that all of their brains are unique and that they can learn and improve their learning. Develop this further by explaining that, when they are learning something new, it can cause the brain to grow new connections between the neurons.

Share with the children your own example of why your brain is fantastic and elastic. It might include statements such as:

- My brain is elastic because I persevered and learnt to ride my bike.
- My neurons are firing in maths because I am learning my six times table.
- My brain can do different things: it can remember facts and learn new things.
- I can make my brain stronger by making mistakes and learning from them.

Bringing it together – what have we learned?

Ask the children to think about their own brain and how fantastic and elastic it is. Explain to the children that they are going to record information about why their own brain is fantastic and elastic (see Figure 72). Reinforce the idea that every brain is unique because they will all have had different learning experiences.

Once the children have completed their recording, randomly select some children to share why their brain is fantastic and elastic. You could use a visualiser to share their ideas. Probe the children's learning further by asking:

Why is that fantastic?

Which learning skills have you used?

What would you like your brain to learn to do next?

This activity can be differentiated through the use of an app such as 'Explain everything', where children can explain why their brains are fantastic and elastic.

Challenge

Ask the children to think about the different parts of the brain – cerebrum, amygdala, hippocampus and cerebellum. Can they explain how each part of their brain is fantastic and elastic?

Further developments

The app 'Your fantastic elastic brain' supports the book and could be used by the children either in school or with parents at home.

Create a class display explaining how the brain is fantastic and elastic.

Children's responses

Which one is the odd one out?

'The elastic band is the odd one out because it doesn't teach you how to learn.'

'Ball is the odd one out because the other two can stretch and grow.'

'The brain is the odd one out as the others are objects.'

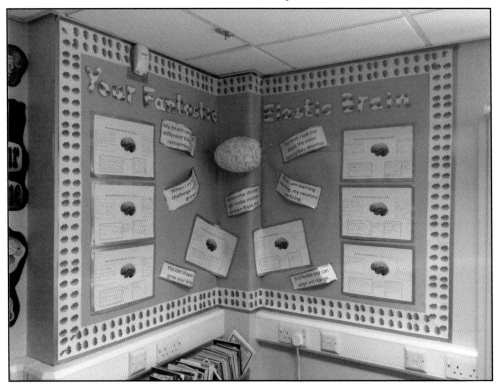

Figure 71 Fantastic elastic brain display

My Fantastic Elastic Brain

When I started handwriting I could hardly write anything but I persevered and I got better, better and better than I still ~~havn't~~ haven't mastered handwriting.

When I first started reading I could hardly read a word but teachers and a assistants helped me and I quickly Got better at reading now I'm amazing at reading.

I didn't like history then I found more about what it's like then Suddenly started to love history and now it's my favourite subject.

When I first started swimming I couldn't Get my 5 metres back done but I got lots of help and my ~~your~~ brain swiftly ~~advanced~~ advanced then I finally did it!

My Fantastic Elastic Brain

I used to take the easy work but now I challenge myself.

I used to be really scared at swimming because I thought that I would sink but now I'm not scared

I used to complain when I had to practice my clarinet but now I like to practice.

I used to get grumpy when I didn't get top marks but now I'm not bothered because I know I can try harder next time.

My Fantastic Elastic Brain

I like to challenge myself and do harder learning. In maths I always like to reach the tricky sheet.

My brain always grows because at the start when I first started swimming I was really scared but now I have really improved.

My brain can remember names, phonenumbers and strangely regplates.

My brain is great because I can do great things in art.

My Fantastic Elastic Brain

In rock Climbing I tryed and tryed to get all my awards and in the end I did it.

In math last year I found it really tricky So I persoverd and did my home work I can do it now.

I had learnt to ride a bike I went up a big hill and I felldown So I tryed again and did it.

I like a challenge.

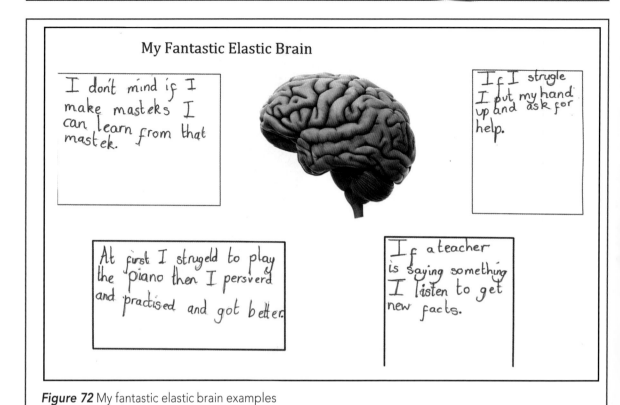

My Fantastic Elastic Brain

I don't mind if I make masteks I can learn from that mastek.

If I strugle I put my hand up and ask for help.

At first I strugeld to play the piano then I persverd and practised and got better.

If a teacher is saying something I listen to get new facts.

Figure 72 My fantastic elastic brain examples

Downloadable resources

PowerPoint presentation 'Which is the odd one out?'
Mindset trumps template
bit.ly/2e3zSk2

6 Learning cereals

Learning objectives	Resources
• To identify the characteristics of an effective learner • To create a design for a learning cereal packaging	• Images of cereal boxes or bags • Materials for design • Tablets (optional) • Visualiser or document camera (optional)

Lesson

1 *Initially, arrange the children so they are sitting with their talk partner and can also clearly see the board. You could provide the children with a range of cereal boxes to stimulate the discussion.*

Ask the children to think and talk about:

How many different things can you think of that we eat for breakfast?

Take feedback and then ask the children to focus on cereals. Ask the children:

Who eats cereal for breakfast? (The children can respond by a show of hands.)

What do you know about cereal?

What do you think makes a good cereal?

Why is cereal important?

What would you include in a good cereal?

Ensure you build in talk time between each question to allow the children to reflect.

Learning cereal

2 Explain to the children that they are going to design a new breakfast cereal that will help them become an effective learner.

Ask them to discuss with their talk partner:

What makes an effective learner?

If your children are not familiar with the characteristics of an effective learner or if you have children who need further support, you could provide them with a range of characteristics on cards for them to sort and to stimulate discussion. You could use the cards from Figure 67 on page 145.

Provide the children with some talk time and then ask them for feedback. Randomly select children to feed back using either lollipop sticks or raffle tickets attached to their chairs.

Explain to the children that they are going to design the cereal box for their new learning cereal and that they need to encourage people to eat it. Look at a range of cereal packet designs and discuss with the children which ones they think are effective and why. Create success criteria for the effective packaging of a learning cereal.

It might also be useful to provide initial scaffolding for the discussion; for example, you could model an idea: **'I would create a cereal that contains extra perseverance to ensure that learners didn't give up.'**

3 The children can then create their cereal packet design using a variety of materials (see Figure 73). Alternatively the children could create their design using an app such as 'Paper 53' or 'Brushes redux'.

Bringing it together – what have we learned?

Randomly select some examples of the children's cereal packaging and share them using a visualiser if you have one. Ask the children to discuss the child's learning and to think about:

What is successful about this design?

How could she or he challenge themselves and improve it?

What are the key ingredients for his or her cereal?

Challenge

Provide the children with some statements and ask them to reflect on whether they make you an effective learner:
● repeatedly making careless mistakes in maths
● checking spelling using a dictionary
● asking a friend for help
● copying someone's work.

Further developments

Children could create a menu for a learning diet that promotes the effective characteristics of a learner.

Children could write an advert to promote their learning cereal and the effective characteristics of learning.

Downloadable resources

Video of children discussing mistakes

bit.ly/2dyhsqO

Children's responses

What makes a successful learner?

    'Concentration'

    'Growth mindset'

    'Making mistakes and learning from them.'

    'Enthusiasm'

    'Imagination'

    'Paying attention.'

    'Not giving up on challenges or things they find hard.'

    'Brain'

    'Asking for help.'

    'Listening carefully.'

    'Creativity'

    'Practising at home and in school.'

What does a successful cereal packaging need?

    'Says on the packet what it does.'

    'A full and healthy breakfast – ready for school.'

    'Balanced'

    'Great logo and characters so children like them.'

    'It should be healthy and list the ingredients.'

Figure 73 A learning cereal

Lessons for 9–10 year olds
(Year 5, UK)

Lesson		Focus	Page
1	Passport to learning	Reflecting on the different mindsets, how they use them and what their strengths are	160
2	Too old to …	Suggesting ways to help someone learn; exploring stereotypes	166
3	What makes a great teacher?	Identifying the characteristics of a successful teacher; justifying opinions	169
4	Brain power!	Creating a 3D model of the brain; explaining how the brain works	179
5	Famous failures	Debating what it means to be a failure; reflecting on how the characteristics of the mindsets affects being successful or being a failure	184
6	The iceberg illusion	Explaining what happens when you are learning; creating images to illustrate the learning process	189

Overview

Children are asked to reflect on how they learn and to develop personal challenges in greater detail in a 'learning passport'. The learning groups are revisited and used to debate whether you can be too old to be a learner. Children are asked to reflect on the role of a teacher in their learning process. The lessons also deepen the children's understanding of the brain as they are required to work collaboratively to make a model brain to share with younger children. Children are asked to further explore the idea of being successful and to use 'sketchnoting' to explore the hidden factors that contribute to success.

1 Passport to learning

Learning objectives	Resources
• To identify the strengths and areas for development in learning • To reflect on when they use different mindsets and how this affects their learning	• Growth and fixed mindset vocabulary cards (Figure 74) • Learning passport template (Figure 75) • Learning passport completed by the teacher

Lesson

1 *Arrange the class so the children are sitting with their talk partner and have a clear view of the board. If you have a visualiser, document camera or tablet ensure these are set up and ready to be used.*

Provide the children with a list of growth and fixed mindset characteristics (Figure 74). Then ask them to read them through and check that they understand all the vocabulary. If there are any words they are uncertain of, build in some talk time to discuss them. Take feedback from the children and clarify any misconceptions.

Ask the children to work with their talk partner to sort the cards into groups. Explain that there are no right or wrong answers and that are you are just interested in their opinions. It would be useful to display these characteristics on the board as it will allow the children to model how they have organised them and allow the other children to feed back.

Randomly select a pair to share how they have sorted the cards. They could model their sort on the board and explain why they have chosen to organise the characteristics in this way.

Probe the children's learning further by asking:

How have you organised the characteristics?

Why did you choose to organise them in that way?

Could you organise them in a different way?

Can you suggest another characteristic that you could add to the group?

What is a growth mindset?

What is a fixed mindset?

likes easy work	likes to be challenged	wants to be right
stops trying if they think something is difficult	likes to be the first to finish	is determined to keep trying
recognises mistakes are part of learning	wants to be a learner	perseveres when learning is difficult

Figure 74 Growth and fixed mindset vocabulary cards (2)

2 In addition to sorting the characteristics that you have provided, the activity could be extended by challenging the children to add their own ideas/behaviours on sticky notes.

Learning passports

3 *You will need to have previously completed your own learning passport to share with the children. Try to be as honest as possible as you need to be a role model for the children. It might be necessary to first have a brief discussion about what a passport is.*

Share your passport with the children. Try to model and explain your rationale behind your thinking, for instance:

'I find it very difficult to have a growth mindset in everything I do as I prefer to do English and enjoy reading.'

'When I am putting effort into something you would see me getting things wrong, sometimes asking for help and trying different ways. I would be trying my best. I could be doing better than I have done previously.'

4 Explain to the children that they are going to complete their own learning passport and that these are not going to be marked. They need to think about themselves as a learner and how they behave and feel. Remind them that the passports are a personal reflection of them as a learner.

Give out the learning passport templates (see Figure 75) and allow the children a few minutes to think about its questions and headings. You could clarify some of the questions such as:

What does it look like when you are putting effort in? (If I walked into classroom and you were doing some learning and putting lots of effort into it, what would it look like?)

Effort

What does it look like when you are putting effort into your work?

How do you feel when you find something difficult or can't do it?

Where do you think you could put more effort in?

What do you do if you can't do something?

Mindset

What type of mindset do you have?

Challenge

What do you find challenging in school?

What level of challenge do you like?

0   10

Can you give me an example of when you have used your growth mindset?

How could you help develop yourself in that area?

How are you challenged in school?

How easy is it to have a growth mindset?

How do you feel when you are being challenged?

Figure 75 Learning passport template

Bringing it together – what have we learned?

Once the children have completed their passports, encourage them to feed back:

How did you feel when you were completing your learning passport?

Is it useful to spend time reflecting on you as a learner?

Have you learned anything about yourself?

Which part of the passport did you find the most challenging to complete?

If you could change the passport in any way, what would you change?

Challenge

Can children create their own version of the learning passport for you to complete? Ask them to think about:

How would you present it?

What subheadings/sections would you include?

Further developments

Throughout the year, the learning passports can be revisited and children might want to use them during lessons. The children should be asked to reflect on the following:

Does the passport still reflect you as a learner?

Has anything changed?

Downloadable resources

Growth and fixed mindset vocabulary cards

Learning passport template

bit.ly/2ebXseS

Children's responses

What is a growth mindset?

'A growth mindset means if there's no one around you choose the right learning behaviour.'

'Fixed mindset is where you don't do anything, you don't challenge yourself. Growth mindset is where you do.'

'Fixed mindset – you think the work is so easy.'

'Fixed mindset chooses easy work and gets it right. Then gets stuck when faced with challenging work.'

'If you get a question wrong and you've failed think of it as your first attempt in learning.'

'If you think having a growth mindset makes you the best, which is like having a fixed mindset and shows you don't understand it.'

Which part of the passport did you find the most challenging to complete?

'The effort section, because when you find something hard it's not always easy to explain why.'

'I found completing my passport challenging. It is hard to be truthful and to reflect on where you are going wrong.'

Did you find it helpful to complete a passport?

'Yes, as the teachers know what you need to improve on.'

'You can look at it in a few years and see how you have improved.'

'It helps you know more about yourself.'

'Yes, as you can get support as the teacher knows.'

'When you're grown up you'll know what you were like when you were younger.'

Mindset

What type of mindset do you have?

I have a growth mindset because when there is no teachers around my leadership starts to shine.

What do you do if you can't do something?

I sometimes scribble it out what I know I have to remember to put one ruler line through it or I leave it alone and take it as part of my work.

Figure 76 My growth mindset

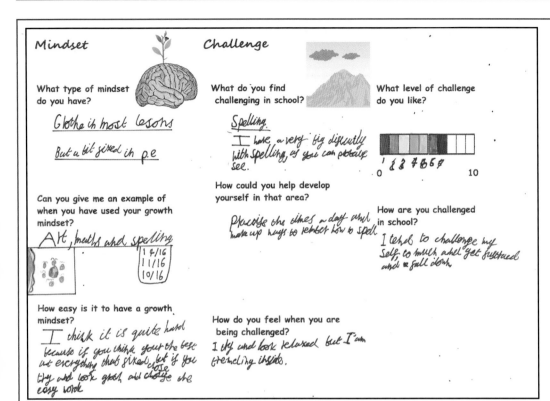

Figure 77 My mixed mindset (1)

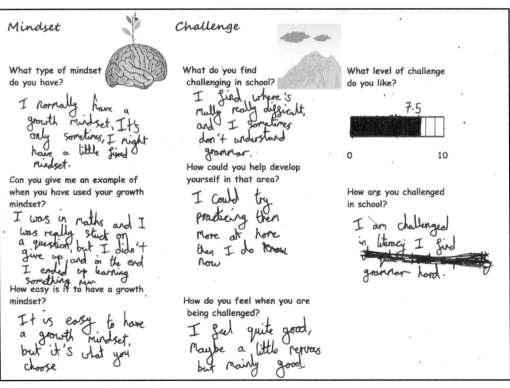

Figure 78 My mixed mindset (2)

2 Too old to …

Learning objectives	Resources
• To suggest ways to help someone learn • To explore stereotypes	• Role badges (optional) • Picture of an elderly person • Picture of a tablet • Some pictures of common stereotypes (see below)

Lesson

1 *Ensure your room is set up to encourage effective discussion between the children. The children are to work in learning groups and will each take on a role. An effective arrangement is square tables with four children sitting two either side facing each other. The tables could be arranged at a slight angle to ensure everyone can clearly see the board.*

Recap/introduce the different roles that the children take on in the learning groups: **manager**, **reporter**, **encourager** and **recorder**. Use the cards or posters from Figure 25 on page 80 if necessary. These roles can be allocated to different children when you use the learning groups or you could give a child a specific role for a sustained period to allow them to develop their skills. You might want two children to share a role, depending on the number of children in your class. The encourager is an ideal role for sharing. The children can also wear badges to reinforce the roles that they are playing.

2 Reveal a picture of an elderly person and a tablet to the class. Explain to the children that they are going to debate in their learning groups:

Is an elderly person too old to learn how to use a tablet?

Put the word '**debate**' on the board and ask the children to discuss as a learning group what they think this word means and how they should behave.

While the discussions are taking place observe the children and, when you think it is an appropriate moment, bring the discussions to a close and ask the groups for feedback. Through careful questioning, reach an agreement on a shared definition of a debate. Examples of possible questions are:

Do you agree a debate is where we …?

What should you do if you disagree with someone's ideas?

Do we have to agree with everyone's ideas?

Will there be a right or wrong answer?

This could be developed further by briefly creating a list of behaviours we should see when a debate is happening, for example, sharing ideas and listening and responding to people's suggestions.

Remind the children that they have to share their opinions but can also to ask questions to challenge each other. You could provide the children with question prompts to encourage them to develop their thinking. Children can choose to record their work in their own format.

3 Ask the children to work in their learning groups to debate whether an elderly person can learn to use a tablet. You could remind the children to think about an elderly person in general rather than the oldest person in the world! It might also be appropriate to have a discussion about what the word '**elderly**' means to avoid any misconceptions. The teacher should act as a facilitator, observing the groups and only intervening when necessary. While listening to the group discussion, take a note of any misconceptions or interesting ideas and feed these into the discussion, by posing a question or returning to them at another point.

To probe and deepen the children's discussions, ask them to think about the following during their discussions. You could reveal these questions on the board once the discussions are underway to extend them further:

Can you think of ideas for and against?

Why do you think that …?

What evidence do you have to support your ideas?

What would a person need in order to be able to learn how to use a tablet?

Before you want the children to feed back, give them a five-minute warning to allow the reporter to prepare. If this is the first time the children have worked in these roles, you could model how to effectively report back to the class.

Bringing it together – what have we learned?

Ask the reporters to feed back on their discussion and the conclusion they came to. Key questions are:

What did you discuss?

Why did your group think that?

Can you expand on your idea further?

What conclusion did you come to?

Was it a difficult decision to make? Why?

Explain that we often have preconceived ideas that affect us and the opinions we have. Often these ideas can be formed based on limited knowledge or how things are represented on the television or through the media. Share some images of these ideas and explain that they are called 'stereotypes'. Ask the children:

Do you know of any other stereotypes?

How can we prevent stereotypes?

Ask each group to nominate a member who they think has improved and put greater effort into their role and learning. Take feedback from the groups and ask them to explain why they have chosen that person.

Challenge

Can the children suggest an alternative question for debate?

Further developments

The class could debate other issues that involve stereotypes such as 'Can a disabled person play sport?' or 'Are girls better cooks?'

Children's responses

Is an elderly person too old to learn how to use a tablet?

Yes

- 'They could be shaky and not able to use it.'
- 'Some people might want to read a book rather than learn to use an iPad.'
- 'It could be dangerous they might get a virus from the iPad.'
- 'The older you get the harder it can be.'
- 'It may be too fragile and they could break it.'
- 'You might keep forgetting things.'

No

- 'An iPad has SIRI so you can use voice control. It doesn't matter if you have shaky hands.'
- 'You are never too old to do anything!'
- 'Old people can do what they want.'
- 'If you are old you may wish to experiment.'
- 'There are apps that can help you.'
- 'You can teach them.'
- 'No, different people can use an iPad for different things.'
- 'You can ask people if you need help.'
- 'They can do what they want.'
- 'Someone can teach you.'

Do you know of any other stereotypes?

- 'Boys can't do ballet.'
- 'Girls can't play football.'
- 'Boys do more dangerous things.'
- 'Girls shouldn't join the army.'

What would a person need in order to be able to learn how to use a tablet?

- 'Someone to help them.'
- 'Patience and perseverance.'
- 'Be determined.'
- 'A growth mindset.'

3 What makes a great teacher?

Learning objectives	Resources
• To identify the characteristics of a successful teacher • To justify their opinions	• Odd one out images (Figure 79) • 'There is no bathroom!' scene from the film *Kindergarten Cop* • Outline of a teacher (see 'Children's responses') • Visualiser, document camera or tablet

Lesson

1 *Arrange the classroom so the children can see the board and are sitting with their talk partner.*

Reveal the images to the children of a school, people playing sport and a learner driver (see Figure 79). Ask them to discuss with their talk partner which is the odd one out. Explain that there is no right or wrong answer and that you are just interested in their opinions.

Allow the children some time to debate while you assume the role of facilitator. Listen carefully to their discussions and pick up on any misconceptions or interesting viewpoints. You could use these to develop the discussion by posing them as questions; for example: '**Do you have to be a certain age before you can learn to …?**'

At an appropriate moment, draw the discussions to a conclusion and take feedback. Probe the children's thinking further by asking:

Which do you think is the odd one out?

Why do you think that?

Can you identify a different odd one out?

Can you suggest another picture that we could add to the group?

Which is the odd one out?

Figure 79 Which is the odd one out?

A great teacher

2   Watch the 'There is no bathroom!' scene from the film *Kindergarten Cop*.
Then explain that the children are going to watch the scene again and must
this time focus on the teacher played by Arnold Schwarzenegger, thinking
about whether he is an effective teacher or not.

Provide the children with some talk time to discuss his behaviour. Take
feedback from the children and probe their thinking further by asking:

How does the teacher behave?

Why do you think he does that?

Do you think that's a good idea?

Is he a great teacher? Why/why not?

You might need to focus discussions beyond that of just the teacher's
behaviour.

3   Explain to the children that you now want them to think about a teacher
who would help them to be the best learner they can be. Provide each
pair with an outline of a teacher and ask them to create a template for an
effective teacher. Remind the children they should think about:

What are the characteristics of an effective teacher?

Why are these important?

How should teachers behave?

How can they help you to learn?

What does a good teacher need to know?

How does a good teacher behave?

What kinds of things do they say?

Bringing it together – what have we learned?

Once the children have completed their designs of an effective teacher, randomly select pairs to share their ideas using a visualiser, document camera or tablet.

After a selection of children have shared their ideas, provide the children with some thinking and talk time to reflect on:

Are all effective teachers the same?

Were there any characteristics that everyone identified?

Are there any characteristics that have not been identified?

Could you be an effective teacher?

Do we, as learners, all need the same type of teacher?

Why does a teacher need a growth mindset?

Challenge

Children could create a job advert for a new teacher at their school. They should think about:

What characteristics are important?

How would you persuade them to apply for the job?

Further developments

It would be useful to share some of the children's ideas with the staff at your school and to provide the teachers with time to discuss and reflect on them.

Downloadable resources

PowerPoint presentation 'Which is the odd one out?'
Perfect teacher template
bit.ly/2ejB6vK

Children's responses

Which is the odd one out?

'The car is the odd one out as others can take place at school.'

'You can't learn to drive at school so the car is the odd one out.'

'When you are driving you are learning how to drive, you get taught to do something and learn in all three.'

'Rugby is the odd one out as you have a coach not a teacher.'

'Are a teacher and a coach the same?'

'A coach could be called a teacher.'

'They are different as a coach only teaches sport; teachers specialise in learning and children.'

How does the teacher behave? (a bad teacher)

'The teacher is terribly behaved, they are shouting at children and not letting them do things.'

'He is out of order and shouting for no reason. The children are young and need encouraging.'

'He is not listening to the children.'

'He needs to explain more.'

'Teachers need to be strict.'

'It gives a bad impression, the children may copy and he should be a role model.'

Why does a teacher need a growth mindset?

'Teachers need one so they don't give up explaining when someone doesn't understand. They need to be patient.'

'They need a growth mindset to challenge themselves and others.'

'They need to persevere and have willpower to keep going and trying as a teacher.'

'As they need to want to learn things rather than being told to.'

What are the effective characteristics that everyone identified? (a good teacher)

'They should be kind but a little strict.'

'They need to encourage children to do their best and challenge themselves.'

'Always there for you.'

'Teachers can be different.'

'Motivated and effective.'

Teachers Wanted!

We need teachers!
Ludworth Primary school ~~have~~ has two vacant teaching spaces. But we need... Perfect× Teachers.

To obtain ~~these~~ these outstanding places you ~~need to~~ must aquire the following:
- You must be,
- A good leader,
- Determined,
- Positive,
- Enthusiastic,
- Fun,
- Kind,
- Contribute to the school,
- Fair,
- Wise
- Sporty
- Confident
- Mildly strict
- Has a growth mindset
- Happy
- Includes everybody

Figure 80 Teachers wanted! (1)

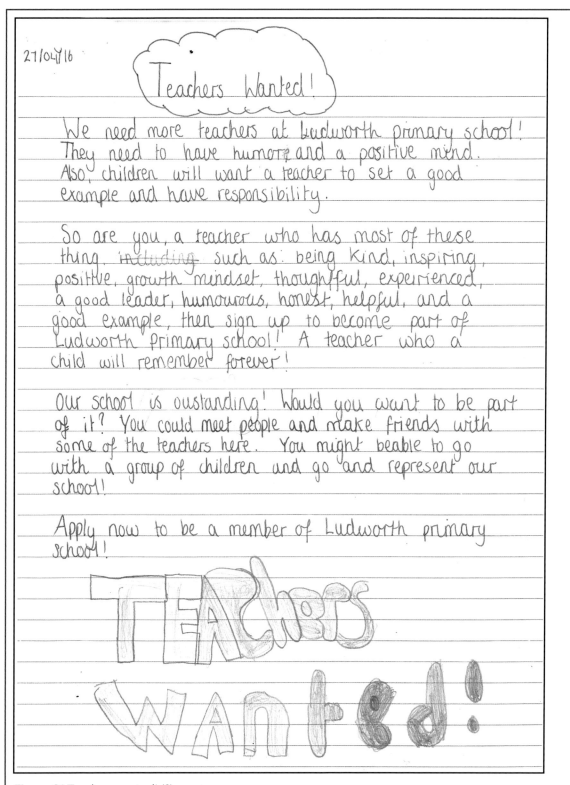

21/04/16

Teachers Wanted!

We need more teachers at Ludworth primary school! They need to have humore and a positive mind. Also, children will want a teacher to set a good example and have responsibility.

So are you, a teacher who has most of these thing, ~~including~~ such as: being kind, inspiring, positive, growth mindset, thoughtful, experienced, a good leader, humourous, honest, helpful, and a good example, then sign up to become part of Ludworth primary school! A teacher who a child will remember forever!

Our school is oustanding! Would you want to be part of it? You could meet people and make friends with some of the teachers here. You might beable to go with a group of children and go and represent our school!

Apply now to be a member of Ludworth primary school!

Figure 81 Teachers wanted! (2)

THE TEACHER

THAT'S NEEDED

We have a vacancy at our school (Ludworth Primary) and we are willing to apply anyone & who is perfect for the job we will be having numerous interviews for this job, you pespiricly have to have the qualitys that are underlined.

The teacher we need must be able to do gymnastics and must be free on a Tuesday and Friday. They also must be able to dance but this time Monday and Thursday. You will have days off Wednesday, Sunday and Saturday.

You must be a good lisener and challenge all the students very well. A good teacher is also firm but fair. You must keep the Kids entertained otherwise they start talking and messing around. You have to have a growth mindset and show good leadership skills.

You need to be trustworthy and follow rules. You must be polite, but humorous at times. A gymnastic teacher is the main one you have to be flexible. I'm expecting a generous, sensible and wise teacher. You must also be clever because you will cover lessons also.

You will be teaching year 5/6

Contact on our website: Ludworth.org.co.uk
Or call me the : 765192 11560

Your, thank you
                    Ludworth's headteacher.

Figure 82 Teachers wanted! (3)

Perfect Teacher

He would be quite strict but not too strict and would shout when it is needed.

He would be encourage children to do their best and challenge pupils.

Does not ever discourage or disengage pupils when they are talking.

Inspires pupils.

Is very understanding of pupils and their theories.

Does Sun and interesting lessons.

Does a ranges of topics.

Be a role model in the school.

He would say inspirational things and always help you is you were stuck.

Treat everyone equally.

Figure 83 The perfect teacher (1)

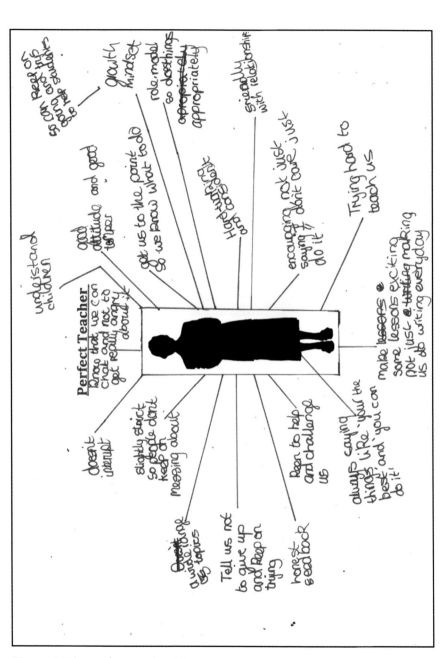

Figure 84 The perfect teacher (2)

Figure 85 The perfect teacher (3)

4 Brain power!

Learning objectives	Resources
• To create a 3D model of the brain • To explain how the brain works	• YouTube clips: youtube.com/watch?v=bLHutEdVEH4 (includes three key areas of the brain) OR youtube.com/watch?v=JuJy1THhqSY (includes different parts of the brain in greater detail) • Images of parts of the brain (Figure 86) • Swimming cap • Shaving foam or similar • Materials to create a 3D brain such as bricks, plasticine, modelling clay, fabric

Lesson

1 *Arrange the children so they are sitting with their talk partner and can see the board.*

   Watch a video clip explaining how the brain works. The two examples listed in the resource list above contain clear explanations that are suitable for children, but the internet has many different examples.

   After watching the clip, ask the children:

   What did you learn from that clip?

   What does the ... do?

   Which part of the brain ...?

2 Ask the children to work with their talk partner to match the images of the different parts of the brain with an explanation of how they work on the whiteboard. Take feedback from the children and correct any misconceptions.

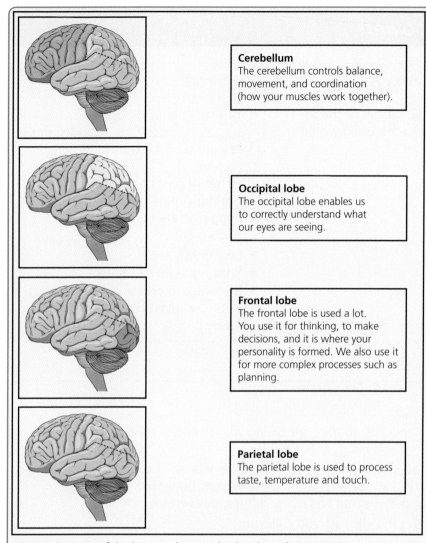

Cerebellum
The cerebellum controls balance, movement, and coordination (how your muscles work together).

Occipital lobe
The occipital lobe enables us to correctly understand what our eyes are seeing.

Frontal lobe
The frontal lobe is used a lot. You use it for thinking, to make decisions, and it is where your personality is formed. We also use it for more complex processes such as planning.

Parietal lobe
The parietal lobe is used to process taste, temperature and touch.

Figure 86 Parts of the brain to be matched with explanations

Model brains

3 Choose a volunteer and explain that you are going to create a brain. Place a cap on the volunteer's head (a swimming cap works well). Using shaving foam, choose a part of the brain and create it on the cap. An alternative way of modelling this would be to use a model of the brain made from a mould (widely available on the internet) using jelly or cake.

Each time, state which part of the brain you are making and ask the children what it does. Repeat for the key parts of the brain:
- cerebrum
- hippocampus
- cerebellum
- amygdala
- prefrontal cortex.

4   Tell the children that they are going to create a model brain using materials of their choice (see Figures 87–90). This will then be used to help explain how a brain works to 6 and 7 year olds. You could share examples of how children have previously made brains from materials such as bricks, wool or modelling clay. Remind the children that the key parts of the brain need to be clear and that they will be receiving feedback from the younger children about how effective their models are.

Give the children time to discuss:

What will you make the brain out of?

Why have you chosen that?

Which parts of the brain will you include?

How would you ensure each part of the brain is easily identified?

5   The children now make their models of brains using any materials they wish.

Bringing it together – what have we learned?

Once the brains are complete, allocate time for the children to share their models with younger children and to receive feedback from them. You could give the younger children a format for giving feedback or base it on success criteria, which the older children could create prior to making their presentation.

Challenge

The children could choose to include additional parts of the brain in their model such as the occipital, insular or parietal lobe.

Further developments

The children could use their models to create short video clips, explaining how the brain works.

A display of the different brains could be created with parts of the brain clearly labelled and including key facts.

Downloadable resources

Powerpoint presentation of parts of the brain to be matched with explanations

bit.ly/2dUJtet

Children's response

Figure 87 A brain made of LEGO® blocks (1)

Figure 88 A brain made of LEGO® blocks (2)

Figure 89 A material brain (1)

Figure 90 A material brain (2)

5 Famous failures

Learning objectives	Resources
• To debate what it means to be a failure • To reflect on how the characteristics of growth and fixed mindsets affects being successful or being a failure	• Role badges (optional) • Picture of prizes (Figure 91) • Photos of Rebecca Adlington at the London 2012 Olympic Games • Headlines from news reports about Rebecca Adlington

Lesson

1 *Children will work in learning groups. Ensure your room is set up to encourage effective discussion between the children. An effective arrangement is square tables with the four children sitting two either side facing each other. The tables could be arranged at a slight angle to ensure everyone can clearly see the board.*

Recap/introduce the different roles that the children work in for the learning groups: **manager**, **reporter**, **encourager** and **recorder**. Use cards or posters as in Figure 25 on page 80 if required. These roles can be allocated to different children when you use the learning groups or you could give a child a specific role for a sustained period to allow them to develop their skills. You could ask two children to share a role depending on the number of children in your class. The encourager is an ideal role for sharing. The children may also wear badges to reinforce the roles that they are playing.

2 Show the children some pictures of prizes, as in Figure 91.

Ask them to discuss:

What do these things all have in common? (You might need to explain the word 'common' or replace it with 'How are they all connected?')

How do you achieve them?

Look at the prizes: which is the most important one to achieve?

To be successful, do you need a prize?

Is a goal the same as a prize?

Select the questions that are appropriate for your children to focus them to reflect on their own motivation.

Figure 91 Examples of prizes

Debate time

3 Explain that the children are going to debate in their learning groups:

Was Rebecca Adlington a failure because she won a bronze medal in the Olympics?

Reveal the word '**debate**' on the board and recap with the children what happens in a debate and the behaviours they agreed on in Year 3 Lesson 3 (page 114).

Remind the children that they have to share their opinions but can also ask questions to challenge each other. Provide the children with question prompts to encourage them to develop their thinking. They can choose to record their work in their own format.

Share some images of Rebecca Adlington at the London 2012 Olympic Games or the headlines from the newspapers at the time including '**Even Adlington is forced to settle for THIRD best as GB swimmers struggle to make waves.**'

Encourage the children to reflect on the headlines. Build in some talk time to allow them to discuss:

How do the headlines portray her?

What image do they create?

How do you think she feels?

4 Ask the children to work in their learning groups to debate whether they believe Rebecca Adlington was a failure. The teacher should act as a facilitator, observing the groups and only intervening when necessary. While listening to the group discussion, take note of any misconceptions or interesting ideas and feed these into the discussion by posing a question or returning to them at another point.

To probe and deepen the children's discussions, ask the children to think about the following during their discussions. You could reveal these questions on the board once the discussions are underway to extend them further:

Can you think of reasons why she could be a viewed as a failure or as a success?

Why do you think that ...?

What evidence do you have to support your ideas?

Before you want the children to feed back, give them a five-minute warning to allow the reporter to prepare.

Bringing it together – what have we learned?

Ensure the children are listening by reminding them that they should listen to each group and then they will be given the opportunity to ask questions. Ask the reporters to feed back on their discussion and their verdict. Key questions can be used as prompts:

What conclusion did you come to?

Why did you decide that?

What did you discuss?

Why did your group think that?

Can you expand on your idea further?

Was it a difficult decision to make? Why?

Ask each group to nominate a member who they think has improved and put greater effort into their role and learning. Take feedback from the groups and ask them to explain why they have chosen that person.

Challenge

Ask the children to reflect further on what motivates them.

Introduce the vocabulary '**intrinsic**' and '**extrinsic**'. Explain to what the words mean and ask the children to identify examples of behaviour that reflect them.

Further developments

The idea of someone being successful but being described as a failure can be identified in a range of contexts, particularly sports. Different scenarios could be debated that are more relevant to your class.

Another stimulating debate can be developed from a team that has lost and how they reacted to their defeat. Often football teams can be a great stimulus.

Downloadable resources

PowerPoint presentation showing prizes

Video of children discussing what a debate is

bit.ly/2dMKHrS

Children's responses

What do these things (prizes) all have in common?

> ❛You can earn them; you have to do something good.❜
>
> ❛You can do different things to earn them.❜
>
> ❛You need to come first to get them.❜

Does everyone agree?

> ❛No, it could be a reward for improving.❜
>
> ❛They all make you happy and encourage you.❜
>
> ❛Other people give you them.❜
>
> ❛It makes you feel that someone has appreciated you.❜

Which is the most important?

> ❛Earning one.❜
>
> ❛Depends on you.❜
>
> ❛I wouldn't want any.❜

How do the headlines portray Rebecca Adlington?

> ❛They say 'just got third' like it's not the best.❜
>
> ❛I wonder if the people who wrote the headline could get a bronze medal in the Olympics.❜
>
> ❛I don't like 'forced' and 'struggled to make'. Just think how many people she beat just to get through the heats.❜
>
> ❛If I won a bronze medal at the Olympics I might be a little disappointed but just to get there in the first place would be an achievement, never mind a bronze.❜
>
> ❛I wouldn't be happy if I was Rebecca and they wrote that.❜

Was Rebecca Adlington a failure because she won a bronze medal in the Olympics?

Yes, she was a failure.

'She let the fans down.'

'Did she try her best?'

'The fans and the public expected more of her.'

'She didn't reach her goal.'

No, she wasn't a failure.

'Perhaps some of the other swimmers performed better on that day.'

'She got a bronze medal and through to an Olympic final which is just absolutely brilliant.'

'Her goal was to do her best and she did.'

'She is not a failure as she tried hard and beat most people.'

'It isn't her getting worse; it is other people getting better.'

'You learn from your mistakes.'

'She should be happy that she got there.'

'People have too high expectations of her.'

'As she tried her best we believe she has won the greatest prize self-satisfaction.'

6 The iceberg illusion

Learning objectives	Resources
• To explain what happens when you are learning • To create images to illustrate the learning process	• An image of an iceberg • The Iceberg Illusion (see Figures 92 and 93) • Tablets • 'Paper by Fifty Three' app or an alternative app

Lesson

This lesson works best using a device and an app to create a sketchnote. Prior to the lesson, ensure the children are familiar with your chosen app and the devices. You need to have the Iceberg Illusion downloaded and ready to use. If you do not have access to devices or apps, the children could complete the lesson by them creating a work of art to illustrate learning using an iceberg.

Sketchnotes are rich visual notes created from a mixture of words, drawings, shapes and images. If the children are unfamiliar with sketchnoting, you might need to spend a previous lesson exploring the different techniques.

This YouTube video provides examples and further information about sketchnoting: youtube.com/watch?v=gY9KdRfNN9w

Sylvia Duckworth's excellent presentation 'Sketchnoting for Beginners' at sylviaduckworth.com/presentations *is a great starting point.*

1 Seat the children so they can see the board.

Using a 'torch tool' allows you to only reveal part of the image of an iceberg, which can then be expanded to slowly reveal the whole image. Ask the children:

What can you see?

Why do you think that?

How would you describe it?

Look at the image. Are you seeing the entire iceberg?

What would it be like if you were stranded on an iceberg?

2 Share with the children the amazing sketchnote created by Sylvia Duckworth to illustrate learning. Explain that 'sketchnoting' is a way of creating visual notes by combining text and images using an app.

Figure 92 The Iceberg Illusion (1), Sylvia Duckworth, July 2015

My iceberg of learning

3   Tell the children that they are going to explain learning using the image of an iceberg and what happens beneath the water. Explain that the top of the iceberg above the water is what happens when you have learned successfully. Below the water is what people do not see, that is all the different factors that enable you to learn effectively.

Before the children begin the activity provide them with some talk time and ask them to think about:

What happens when you are learning?

What don't people see when you are successful?

What do you need to do to be successful?

What images could you use to represent ...?

4   Give the children time to create their sketchnote based on a blank copy of Sylvia Duckworth's original (see Figure 92), using an app.

Bringing it together – what have we learned?

Randomly select children to share their icebergs and ask them to explain their creations. Once you have reviewed a selection ask the children to think about:

What are the key characteristics of learning?

Which image do you think illustrates ... effectively?

Is there anything else you think you should add?

You could also share Sylvia Duckworth's original image (see Figure 93) and compare it to the children's ideas. Her original image is available to download from flickr.com/photos/sylviaduckworth

Figure 93 The Iceberg Illusion (2), Sylvia Duckworth, July 2015

Challenge

Ask the children to think about how we could make the invisible aspects of learning (that is, the ones people do not always see such as persistence) more visible in the classroom. Discuss how people can be helped to understand how important they are.

Further developments

The children's ideas could be collated and used to create a giant version of 'The Iceberg Illusion'.

The children could develop their sketchnoting skills to illustrate different aspects of their learning and mindsets.

Downloadable resources

Blank version of Sylvia Duckworth's 'The Iceberg Illusion'
bit.ly/2dYT4Ac

Children's responses

Why is it an iceberg?

> 'Because it is very white like an iceberg.'
>
> 'It's an unusual shape.'

How would you describe an iceberg?

> 'Rugged, uneven and very cold.'
>
> 'Icebergs can float.'
>
> 'When you look at an iceberg you don't see all of it. Most of it is under water.'
>
> 'A body of ice, half submerged in water and it has been broken off from a glacier.'
>
> 'It's like a giant iceberg.'

What do you need to do to be successful?

> 'Sometimes you make mistakes and fail.'
>
> 'Put lots of effort in and try your hardest.'
>
> 'Try new challenges and work hard.'
>
> 'You need an inspiration.'
>
> 'Practise in different ways.'

What images could you use to represent ...?

> 'A shooting star could represent inspiration.'
>
> 'A superhero could represent inspiration.'
>
> 'A red cross could represent a mistake.'
>
> 'A brain working out could represent how you have to work hard.'

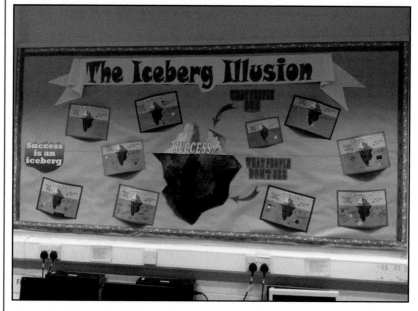

Figure 94 The Iceberg Illusion display

Figure 95 Child's version of The Iceberg Illusion (1)

Figure 96 Child's version of The Iceberg Illusion (2)

Lessons for 10–11 year olds
(Year 6, UK)

Lesson		Focus	Page
1	'Don't say … Say …'	The impact of words and phrases on mindsets; creating effective phrases for learning feedback	196
2	Diamond minds	Identifying what is important for them as an individual learner; identifying barriers to their learning and how they might overcome them using the diamond nine array	201
3	Barriers to learning	Identifying and overcoming barriers to learning using a rock image	207
4	Brain v calculator	Discussing whether a calculator is better than a brain; justifying their opinions and reflecting on the opinions of others	211
5	Mathematical mistakes	Describing how mistakes can help us learn; identifying how we should respond to them	215
6	Learning pathways	Defining learning; creating a way of explaining learning to younger children	219

Overview

Mathematical mistakes are a key focus in Year 6 and this links closely to classroom learning. Children are encouraged to think about how they respond to these mistakes. They are also asked to reflect on the language used to encourage people to learn and on the role of parents. The effective characteristics of a learner are revisited and children are encouraged to reflect on those that enable them to be a learner. Children are also given the opportunity to create their own way of illustrating learning, which could be used to explain learning to younger children.

1 'Don't say... Say...'

Learning objectives	Resources
• To discuss the effects that different types of feedback can have • To create effective phrases for learning feedback	• YouTube video 'Clever girl' at youtube.com/watch?v=VAMQs1tjlM4 • Feedback grid (Figure 97)

Lesson

1 *Arrange the children so they are sitting with their talk partner and can clearly see the board.*

Watch the YouTube video 'Clever girl'. Ask the children to think about:

What did you hear and see in the video?

Why do you think a parent would say 'clever girl/boy' to their child?

Explain to the children that you want them to think about and then to discuss with their talk partner:

Do you think it is a good idea to praise a baby by saying 'Clever girl!' or 'Clever boy!'?

Why do you think that?

Explain that you are interested in their opinions and the reasons why they have those opinions. Remind the children that they might have different opinions but it is important to listen to different viewpoints.

When you feel the children's discussion has reached an appropriate point, ask the children to feed back whether they think it is a good idea and to share their reasons.

2 Develop the discussion further by asking the children to think about the following questions:

What does the word 'clever' mean to you?

Should we tell someone they are clever?

Do you like being told you're clever? Why?

Is it good to praise children?

It might be useful to display these key questions on a whiteboard to allow the children to focus their discussions on the key points. Take feedback from the children.

'Don't say... Say ...'

3 Explain that research shows that 'false praise' or excessive praise has a negative effect on learners as it can lead to them needing large amounts of praise as the motivation to do anything, and they can also become extremely reluctant to make mistakes.

Ask the children to talk to their talk partners about alternative ideas:

What should we say instead of 'clever girl/boy' when someone succeeds at something?

Share examples of feedback.

4 Ask the children to discuss which of these helps them to be a better learner: '**Fabulous writing!**' OR '**Fabulous writing. You have carefully chosen words to describe the character.**'

During the talk time the teacher should observe and listen to the children's ideas and any misconceptions. A useful strategy is to turn the misconceptions into questions to allow all children to reflect and discuss them. This allows peer-to-peer support and is extremely powerful.

The following are examples of children's suggestions and ways that they can be addressed by the teacher:

Possible misconception	Teacher's response
Intelligent girl	Is that the same as saying 'clever girl'?
Well done!	What are we praising them for? How have they been successful? Be specific! Well done, you have successfully used connectives to extend your sentences.
Great work!	How does this help you to be a better learner?

5 Provide each child with a feedback grid (Figure 97). Ask them to create a feedback phrase that promotes a growth mindset for each phrase they have been given. Explain to the children that there are no right or wrong answers, just their ideas.

Name: _____	Date: _____
Don't say …	**Say …**
Clever boy/girl	
Well done!	
Well done, you finished that work quickly.	
Wow, that was easy work!	

Figure 97 'Don't say … Say …' feedback grid

Bringing it together – what have we learned?

Look at examples of the children's feedback. Then ask them to work in the two roles of teacher and child. Role play giving both types of feedback to each other. Initially, you could model this yourself with a child or teaching assistant, especially if your children are unfamiliar with giving feedback to each other.

Ask the children to discuss and reflect on:

How do the different types of feedback make you feel?

Which do you think would be more effective? Why?

Challenge

Provide the children with the opportunity to review their books (possibly from the previous year) and to reflect on their own learning:

What was the best feedback you had? Why?

What was the worst feedback you had? Why?

Further developments

Create a display of feedback phrases for the children to use when working with a partner.

Create short video clips of children giving effective feedback. These can be used with younger children, shared with parents and given to staff to reflect on.

Downloadable resources

'Don't say... Say...' feedback grid template

bit.ly/2dOEtew

Children's responses

Why would a parent say 'clever girl/boy' to their child?

❝If you say clever girl, they will want to do it again.❞

❝They might say it if they do something they don't expect them to do.❞

❝It's good praise.❞

❝When they have learnt something new.❞

❝To encourage them.❞

Is it a good or bad idea to say 'clever girl'?

It's a good idea because ...

❝It helps them know it's a good thing.

We praised my baby sister this morning because she sat up on her own. We wanted her to do it again so we made a fuss.❞

It's a bad idea because...

❝They may think they are clever when they are older and they could become boastful.❞

❝They might think they don't need to work.❞

❝In the story of the Hare and the Tortoise, everyone thought the hare was the fastest and he boasted how he was the best. He became too confident and stopped trying.❞

What does the word clever mean?

❝Smart❞

❝You're good at things and intelligent.❞

❝You know a lot of things.❞

Name: _____	Date: _____
Don't say …	Say …
Clever boy/girl	Good try, next time you need to challenge yourself by … Begin with good try; then change your words as you improve. So you have feedback that shows how you are learning.
Well done!	Well done, you have used … in your writing. It's a bit empty maybe try using more meaningful words that say why it was good. Well done on achieving …
Well done, you finished that work quickly.	Specific information on how to get better. Try saying something more beneficial, than encouraging them to rush.
Wow, that was easy work!	That's really good. Do you need something more challenging? You have learnt to do this, we will find you a new learning challenge. This encourages them to pick easy work, try to encourage them to challenge themselves.

Figure 98 Example filled-in 'Don't say… Say…' feedback grid

2 Diamond minds

Learning objectives	Resources
• To identify what is important for them as an individual learner • To identify barriers to their learning and how they might overcome them	• YouTube clip of neurons firing at youtube.com/watch?v=t3TaMU_qXMc • The brain growing picture (see Figure 99) • Blank diamond nine (Figure 100) • Characteristics of being an effective learner cards (Figure 101)

Lesson

1 Arrange the children so they are sitting with their talk partner and can see the board.

Watch the YouTube clip, ensuring that the title of the clip is hidden.

Ask the children to discuss with their talk partner what they think they have just watched. Then take feedback and, if necessary, explain that they have just watched the neurons inside the brain firing as they receive and send information during the learning process.

2 Develop this further by explaining to the children that, as you learn, the brain makes connections and grows. The brain's capacity increases and it becomes more complex as it learns new things: as if you were adding extra memory to a computer. In this case it was shown as buying extra memory for your brain. The more we learn, the more connections are made. For instance, look at this (show Figure 99).

Did you know that people who learn to play a musical instrument have a larger auditory center than normal?

The 'sound' area of the brain developed more connections as they learnt new things.

Figure 99 The brain grows with learning

Diamond minds

3 Share with the children the blank 'diamond nine' as shown in Figure 100, explaining that it is a means of organising information in order of importance. The most important item should be placed on top and then the next. Some items can be given equal importance and grouped in twos or a three.

Figure 100 The diamond nine

4 Read through the **nine potential characteristics** of being an effective learner as shown in Figure 101. Recap on the meaning of any words that might be unfamiliar.

teacher	feedback	resilience
challenge	effort	knowledgea
a quiet classroom	making mistakes	growth mindset

Figure 101 The characteristics of being an effective learner

5 The children should now create their own 'diamond nine of learning' using a blank diamond nine and nine characteristics cards. Ask them to arrange the nine characteristics into their own order to show which is the most important for them as an individual to be an effective learner (see Figure 102).

It is helpful if the characteristics have been cut out ready so the children do not think they are in a preconceived order. The children can stick them on to the blank template to help them see the structure of a diamond nine clearly. You could add images to the vocabulary cards to support children's understanding.

Explain to the children that there are no right or wrong answers as everyone is a unique learner.

Bringing it together – what have we learned?

Once the children have completed the task, ask them to share their diamond nine of learning with their talk partners. To encourage discussion, you could share some questions they can ask each other:

How did you feel about ordering the different aspects? Was it an easy task?

Why have you chosen this aspect as the most important?

Which was the hardest thing to decide?

Were there any elements that you thought were barriers to your learning?

How would you overcome them?

During the discussions the teacher should act as a facilitator, listening to the discussions and collecting ideas to feed back to the whole class.

Ask some of the pairs to feed back on their discussions and how they created their diamond nines. Discuss with the class how the information can be used to help improve teaching and learning in the classroom.

Select a common aspect that the children have identified as important, such as knowledge or the teacher, and ask the children to discuss whether this is the most important factor.

Challenge

Remove the diamond nine template and ask children to again arrange the characteristics in order of importance. The opened-ended nature of this should allow the children creativity and encourage them to justify their opinions.

Ask the children to work in pairs and, between them, to decide which are the most important aspects. Remind them that they will need to **negotiate**, **compromise** and **persuade**.

Ask the children to select an aspect that is a barrier to their learning and represent it pictorially, for example, as a rock. They can then identify ways to overcome this barrier as an aide-memoire to learning.

Further developments

Give the children a blank diamond nine and ask them to create their own for the different aspects of being an effective learner, trying to add some characteristics that have not be used in the lesson if possible.

Ask the children:

Is there anything you would want to change or add to the diamond nine?

Why is that an important aspect?

Which one do you think would be the most important for you as a learner?

Create a display board that reinforces the different characteristics of an effective learner and having a growth mindset.

Begin to praise children for their learning using the terminology for an effective learner. Praise the process and effort rather than the outcome.

Downloadable resources

PowerPoint presentation about the brain growing with learning

Diamond nine template

Characteristics of being an effective learner cards

Video of children discussing what learning is

bit.ly/2dZJK15

Children's responses

What did you see?

> *The messages in your brain telling you what to do, for example, move your arm.*

> *Neurons firing – they are things in your brain that send messages to your body.*

What does resilience mean?

> *Doing it again and again and never stopping till you succeed.*

> *Showing determination, it doesn't necessarily mean you will succeed but you will keep trying.*

How did you feel about ordering the characteristics? Was it an easy task?

> *It was quite hard because they are all important. They are all things you need.*

> *Difficult, as you have to think about learning and what I do. Often when I am learning I don't think about that I focus on the task.*

Which is the most important characteristic?

> *Making mistakes – if you make a mistake you can learn from it, you can overcome it.*

> *Challenge – if you don't challenge yourself you are not learning.*

> *Effort – I think even if you don't do well in a test or can't do something. If you've put effort into what you are doing, you can still be proud.*

What are the barriers to learning?

> *Quiet classrooms because sometimes you need to talk about learning.*

> *Yes, I want to share my thoughts, or listen to others and be inspired.*

Can you rearrange the characteristics in a different way to represent your learning?

> *As a square, as they are all equally important.*

> *In a line, in order of importance.*

> *You could arrange them to show how they are connected.*

> *As an upside down triangle, with the most important factor at the bottom and then the others layered on top.*

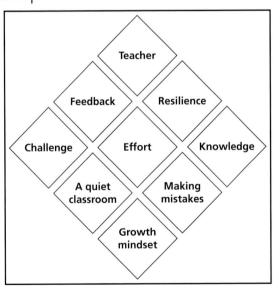

Figure 102 What's important to be an effective learner

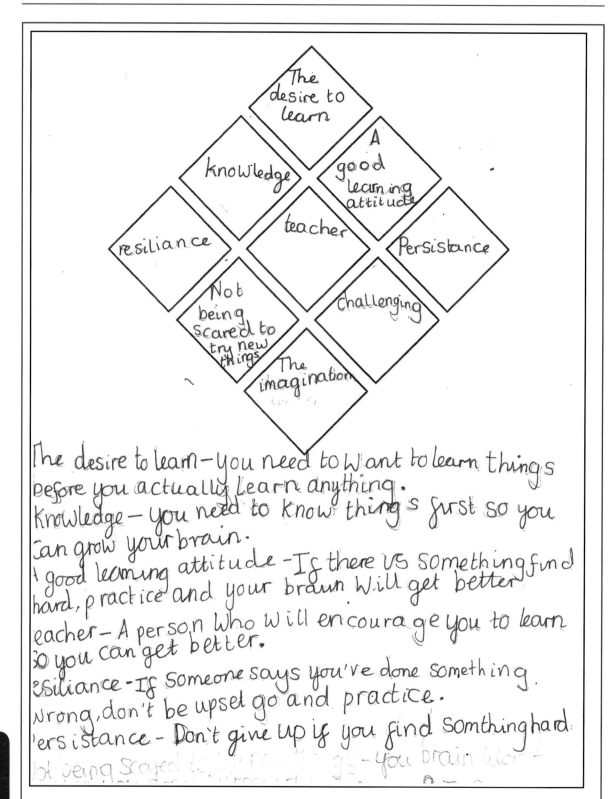

The desire to learn – You need to want to learn things before you actually learn anything.
Knowledge – you need to know things first so you can grow your brain.
A good learning attitude – If there is something find hard, practice and your brain will get better
teacher – A person who will encourage you to learn so you can get better.
resiliance – If someone says you've done something wrong, don't be upset go and practice.
Persistance – Don't give up if you find something hard.
Not being Scared

Figure 103 The desire to learn is most important

3 Barriers to learning

Learning objectives	Resources
• To identify barriers to learning • To identify strategies to help children overcome their barriers to learning	• A picture of a large rock (see Figure 104) • An example of a comic strip (see Figures 106 and 107) • Access to tablets or laptops to create a comic strip (see suggestions of apps below)

Lesson

1 *Seat the children with their talk partners, all with a clear view of the board.*
Together look at the image of a rock in Figure 104, which represents a barrier to a child's learning.
Ask the children to talk with their talk partner and think about:
Why has the rock been chosen to represent a barrier to learning?
What could the rock represent as a barrier for your learning? Why?
How can you overcome barriers to learning?
Take feedback from the children.

Figure 104 The rock barrier to learning

2 Next ask them to reflect on what might be a personal barrier to their own learning. Probe this further by asking them to think about:
Is the barrier related to a specific subject?
What strategies have you tried to overcome it?
Why do you think it's a barrier?

What other strategies could you try?

Again, take feedback from the children.

3 Now ask the children to think about whether the barriers to their learning are **internal** or **external**.

You could provide the children with an example to highlight the differences. For instance, children often state that other people talking is a barrier to their learning. This is an external barrier and, while you can discourage others from talking, you cannot necessarily stop them. An example of an internal barrier could be a child's reluctance to ask for help when they are stuck. They may be reluctant to ask for help, as they are afraid of looking bad in front of their peers.

Barriers to my learning

4 Explain to the children that they are going to create a comic strip to illustrate a barrier to their learning and ways they can overcome it. You could share a range of examples of children's ideas that they have set in different contexts, including the ones shown in 'Children's responses' on page 210.

The children can record their comic strips on a simple framework (see Figure 105) that they draw first, or they could use an app or website to create them.

Figure 105 Framework for a comic strip

Possible apps and websites you could use:
- Make Beliefs Comix: makebeliefscomix.com
- Comic Book: 3dtopo.com/apps/comicbook
- Toon Toolkit: available on the iTunes App Store
- Marvel Kids 'Create your own comic': marvel.com/games/play/34/create_your_own_comic
- Pixton: pixton.com
- ToonDoo: toondoo.com

Bringing it together – what have we learned?

Review the children's comic strips and the different strategies they have used to overcome barriers to their learning. Encourage them to use a wide range of strategies by asking the class to discuss what other ways they can suggest to help their friends overcome their individual rocks/their barriers to learning.

Potential suggestions could include:

- Don't give up.
- Ask a partner for help.
- Understand it's part of the learning process.
- Try again.
- Learn a new strategy.
- Revisit your learning.
- Work in a small group to practise.
- Ask a teacher for help.
- Practise an earlier stage.

Challenge

Provide scenarios where the children make mistakes and fail. Then ask them to role play what they would do. They could be given specific roles such as the teacher, child or friend. Use the context of school for some of the scenarios, but provide other real-life contexts as well.

Further developments

Create a class display of a comic strip featuring a child using a range of strategies to overcome barriers to learning. Include the children's creations.

Downloadable resources

PowerPoint presentation 'Why would you use a rock to represent a barrier to learning?'

Framework for a comic strip

Examples of children's comic strips

bit.ly/2dyhQWm

Children's responses

Why would you use a rock to represent a barrier to your learning?

Because rocks are very hard and you need to challenge yourself to move a rock.

Rocks can block pathways and some can be easier to move then others.

In your learning, what barrier to learning does a rock represent? Why?

A person talking is a rock as it can distract me.

Your attitude can be a rock. As if you think you can't do something and don't try this stops you learning. You're not in the right mindset.

'If you are worried about making mistakes this can be a rock and a barrier to learning.'

Figure 106 Building confidence

Figure 107 What to do if I don't know the answer

This comic strip was created at MakeBeliefsComix.com. Go there to make one yourself!

Figure 108 Example of a child's comic strip, MakeBeliefsComix.com

4 Brain v calculator

Learning objectives	Resources
• To discuss whether they think a calculator is better than a brain • To justify their opinions and reflect on the opinions of others	• Role badges (optional)

Lesson

1 *The children should work in their learning groups. Ensure your room is set up to encourage effective discussion between the children. An effective arrangement is square tables with the four children sitting two either side facing each other. The tables could be arranged at a slight angle to ensure everyone can clearly see the board.*

Recap/introduce the different roles that the children work in for the learning groups: **manager**, **reporter**, **encourager** and **recorder**. Use the materials from Figure 25 on page 80 if required. These roles can be allocated to different children when you use the learning groups or you could choose to give a child a specific role for a sustained period to allow them to develop their skills. Two children could share a role, depending on the number of children in your class. The encourager is an ideal role for sharing. The children can also wear badges to reinforce the roles that they are playing.

2 Explain to the children that they are going to debate in their learning groups:

Is the calculator better than your brain? Why?

Reveal the word '**debate**' on the board and ask the children to discuss as a learning group what they think this word means and how you should behave when debating.

While the discussions are taking place, observe the children and when you think it is an appropriate moment bring the discussions to a close and ask the groups for feedback. Through careful questioning reach agreement on a shared definition of a debate. Possible questions to develop this are:

Do you agree a debate is where we …?

What should you do if you disagree with someone's ideas?

Do we have to agree with everyone's ideas?

Will there be a right or wrong answer?

This could be developed further by briefly creating a list of behaviours we should see when a debate is happening, such as sharing ideas, listening and responding to people's suggestions. If you have already made such a list, refer to it here.

Remind the children that they have to share their opinions but can also ask questions to challenge each other. You could provide the children with question prompts to encourage them to develop their thinking. Children can choose to record their work in their own format.

Brain v calculator

3 Ask the children to work in their learning groups and debate whether a calculator is better than their brain. The teacher should act as a facilitator, observing the groups and only intervening when necessary. While listening to the group discussion, note any misconceptions or interesting ideas and feed these into the discussion by posing a question, or return to them at another point.

To probe and deepen the children's discussions, ask the children to think about the following during their discussions. You could reveal these questions on the board once the discussions are underway to extend them further:

Can you think of ideas for and against?

Why do you think that …?

What evidence do you have to support your ideas?

Before you want the children to feed back, give them a five-minute warning to allow the reporter to prepare. If this is the first time the children have worked in these roles, you could model how to effectively report back to the class.

Bringing it together – what have we learned?

Ask the reporters to feed back their discussion and their verdict. Key questions are:

What did you discuss?

Why did your group think that?

Can you expand on your idea further?

What conclusion did you come to?

Was it a difficult decision to make? Why?

Ask each group to nominate a member who they think has improved and put greater effort into their role and learning. Take feedback from the groups and ask them to explain why they have chosen that person.

Challenge

Ask the children to think about how we could find out whether the brain or the calculator is better. They could create a plan for an investigation using the model they use in science lessons.

Further developments

If the children design a plan to investigate whether the brain or the calculator is best, you could then explore this as a class. For instance, using the idea of multiplying by 10: which is quicker, the calculator or the brain?

An alternative debate could be the brain versus the computer. Which is better?

Downloadable resources

Video of children comparing a brain with a calculator

bit.ly/2dOEJug

Children's responses

What is a debate?

' It's a civilised argument where you tell each other your points.'

' It's a competition where you try to make your point.'

Brain v calculator

Brain	Calculator
If you don't have a brain you can't work a calculator.	A calculator only knows about maths, it doesn't know about anything else.
The brain can do a simple calculation such as 7 × 7 quicker than a calculator.	A calculator can't read or write.
The brain invented the calculator.	A calculator is a lazy way of learning.
The brain can say things instantly but you have to type things into a calculator to come up with an answer.	A calculator is quick and fast.
	A calculator is always reliable.
You can learn and challenge yourself with a brain.	It is small and light.
	It doesn't get fatigued.
A brain is more efficient.	A calculator is useful if you don't have paper.
You can train your brain but not a calculator.	
The brain can think more, it even lets you dream.	You need a calculator for more complex calculations.
The brain can fix a calculator, a calculator can't fix a brain!	The calculator is faster.
	The calculator is easier, more efficient and quicker.
Brains can grow and develop as you learn.	A calculator doesn't change.

During the debate the children also posed questions as part of their response

'*Does a calculator understand or has it just learnt a method?*'

'*Which came first the brain or the calculator?*'

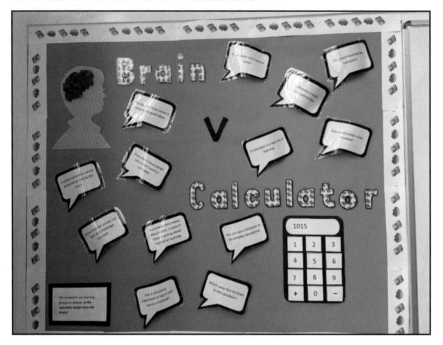

Figure 109 Brain v calculator display

5 Mathematical mistakes

Learning objectives	Resources
• To describe how mistakes can help us to learn • To identify how we should respond to a mistake	• Mathematical mistakes (Figure 110) • Video of Dr. Jo Boaler at vimeo.com/103853269

Lesson

1 *Arrange the children so they are sitting with their talk partner and have a clear view of the board and the teacher.*

Share a calculation with the children and explain that you have completed it. You can use Figure 110 or make up your own to match what the children are learning at the moment.

In the examples that you provide, it is important to model the steps that you have gone through to solve the calculation (ensure some aspects are correct and some include mistakes). This will stimulate discussion and allow the children to identify specifically where you went wrong. You could also share examples of mistakes that the children are making in their learning.

Ask the children to look at your calculation and to discuss and then feed back whether you have been successful or not. Probe their understanding further by asking:

What mistake did I make?

Why do you think I got the wrong answer?

How does this help you as a learner?

How can it help a teacher?

My maths	My maths
What is 27% of £180? 10% is £18 25% is £45 (20% is £36 and 5% is £9) 1% is £1.80 The answer is £46.80	Fred has £180 which is $\frac{2}{5}$ of his money. How much money does Fred have altogether? 180 divided by 5 is 36 36 × 2 = 72 He has £72 altogether.

Figure 110 Examples of mathematical mistakes

2 Repeat for a different calculation.

Learning from mistakes

3 This lesson introduces Jo Boaler and her work to the children. Tell the children that Dr Jo Boaler is a British education author and a Professor of Mathematics Education at the Stanford Graduate School of Education in California. She is involved in promoting mathematics education reform and helping develop mathematical mindsets.

Watch the YouTube clip of Dr Boaler discussing Maths and mistakes.

Ask the children:

What did you learn from the video clip?

Do you think that you are born to be good at maths?

Do your parents believe that they were better at one subject at school?

Do your parents say there was a subject they found hard at school?

How do you feel about making mistakes?

Does your attitude to mistakes change depending on the subject?

4 Share the quote below from Jo Boaler in which she explains what happens when we make a mistake in our learning:

> When teachers ask me how this can be possible, I tell them that the best thinking we have on this now is that the brain sparks and grows when we make a mistake, even if we are not aware of it, because it is a time of struggle; the brain is challenged and the challenge results in growth.

(Available at youcubed.org/think-it-up)

5 Revisit the mistakes that you shared with the children at the start of the lesson and ask them to discuss what type of mistake they think they were:

Were my mistakes part of the learning process or careless mistakes?

Then, at an appropriate point when the children are ready, ask them for feedback.

Probe the children's thinking further by asking them to think about the following questions. You could display them on a board and slowly reveal a question when it is appropriate or have them as a question prompt on the tables:

Which mistakes do you make?

Which type of mistakes helps us to develop as a learner?

What can we do to avoid making careless mistakes?

Bringing it together – what have we learned?

Explain that research shows that mistakes are an important part of the learning process and, depending on how we respond, they can help us learn. Ask the children to think about and discuss how we can ensure that our classroom culture and how we act allows us to make mistakes and learn from them. Ask the children to talk to their partner and discuss:

How can we create a classroom culture that supports mistakes as part of the learning process?

What can you do to help?

What could a teacher do to develop this?

What needs to change?

Challenge

You could widen the discussions and ask the children to think about how we can create a school culture that supports making mistakes as part of the learning process.

Further developments

Share some of the sayings that are used to explain how mistakes are part of the process of learning, for example, '**fail and sail**', which can be written to form acrostics (see 'Children's responses').

Can the children create their own acrostics (see examples below)? You could develop this further by asking the children to illustrate them, for example, as a sketchnote.

Create a class display analysing a mistake in maths and include QR codes that link to video clips of the children discussing mistakes.

Use mistakes in lessons: they can be a great warm-up to ignite children's thinking.

Downloadable resources

PowerPoint presentation with examples of mathematical mistakes

bit.ly/2deqNmN

Children's responses

How does this mistake help you as a learner?

> 'When you make mistakes you learn and improve.'

> 'You can see what to do.'

> 'If you learn from mistakes, you have a growth mindset.'

How can it help a teacher?

‘If I make a mistake, you know what to teach me next.’

‘Teachers can now help you.’

‘If you copy, it doesn't help you learn.’

‘They show teachers what you need help in to improve.’

What can children do to develop a classroom culture that supports mistakes as part of the learning process?

‘Children can share their mistakes. Don't hide them.

‘Some mistakes are careless ones and we should avoid making those.’

‘Other people can support you, by not laughing if you make a mistake.’

‘Other children can explain how to do something and help you learn.’

‘Don't show off!’

Acrostics

Lets	**B**egin
Educate	**A**ttempt
And	**N**umerous tries/**N**ever give up
Revise	**G**o again
Numeracy	

6 Learning pathways

Learning objectives	Resources
• To give opinions on what we mean by the term 'learning' • To create a way of explaining learning to younger children	• The brain working as we learn (see Figure 111) • Forest pathway photographs (see Figure 112)

Lesson

1 *Arrange the children so they are sitting with their talk partner and have a clear view of the board and the teacher.*

Ask the children to discuss with their talk partner what they think we mean by the word 'learning'.

If children require further scaffolding, ask:

Think of something you are good at – something that you know you do well. Discuss how you became good at this.

Think of something that you did in fact learn successfully, but at the time you did not want to learn it. Maybe it is something that you are now glad you learned. What kept you at it?

Take feedback and probe the children's thoughts further by asking questions such as:

Why do you think that?

Can you give a personal experience that reflects that?

Can you explain what happens in the brain when we are learning?

2 Explain to the children how the brain works when we are learning using Figure 111. Explain that there are roughly 150000 km (or more) of neural networks in the human brain and 150000 km is similar to travelling approximately four times round the Earth, as it is approximately 40000 km to travel around it once.

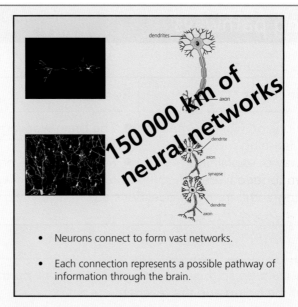

- Neurons connect to form vast networks.

- Each connection represents a possible pathway of information through the brain.

Figure 111 How the brain works when we are learning

Learning pathways

3   Show the children the images of a forest and how a pathway is created (Figure 112). The three images show the creation of a pathway through the wood over time.

Ask the children to discuss with their talk partner how these images relate to learning. Ask them to think about:

Do you think the images reflect learning effectively?

Why do the images represent learning effectively?

Is there anything you would add to illustrate learning more effectively?

Take feedback from the children and use questioning to probe the learning further.

Figure 112 Creating forest pathways

4 Explain to the children that, over a series of lessons, their task is to create a way of illustrating and explaining learning to younger children. Provide them with the time and materials to discuss and plan how they could do this. Allow the children to work independently and observe them discussing and creating their ideas.

Bringing it together – what have we learned?

Ask the children to feed back their discussion and possible ways of explaining learning to younger children. Key questions are:

What did you discuss?

Why did your group think that?

How could you make sure it was accessible to children aged 7?

Ask each group to nominate a member who they think has improved and put greater effort into their role and learning.

Challenge

Ask the children to think about any potential challenges to their idea.

Further developments

This activity could also be linked to the children's transition to secondary school. They could reflect on the challenges they might face and how these might impact on their mindset.

Downloadable resources

PowerPoint presentation about how the brain works during learning, including forest pathways imagery

Video of children discussing the creation of the forest pathway

bit.ly/2ev4ZIA

Children's responses

What does learning mean?

> 'When you understand, you know what it is. Learning is the process you go through to learn, to understand something. It's not always an easy process.'

> 'You start off with a small circle when you're not really good at something. Every time you learn something new you get a bigger circle and you know it.'

> 'Learning means challenging yourself to do more. Practising what you are doing. The challenge is personal to you.'

> 'Developing new skills to make your brain bigger.'

> 'Learning is when if I've made a mistake I could unpick it, and then I would know not to make the mistake again.'

> 'Learning can be knowledge and a skill. Learning to ride a bike is a skill. Learning algebra is knowledge.'

Looking at the images of the forest, can you explain how these can reflect learning and the learning process?

> 'When the trees are all tangles and it was messy and all over the place you could metaphorically speaking have a rope. That rope could be a skill to learn something new. You also need a growth mindset to conquer it. Because if you didn't and you just gave up, you'd be stuck in the mess of weeds.'

> 'At the end of the final image you could have a blockage and you have to clear it. Once you've cleared it, you may need to clear it again to ensure you learn. You keep doing that for the rest of your life.'

> 'An animation could be added. There's a baby on the path, it is a narrow path, as you get older and learn more the path gets bigger. You come to a fork in the road where there are two different paths. You can either go on the fixed mindset path and give up on the problem. Or go down the growth mindset path and find out what you need to know.'

How can you explain learning to younger children?

> 'Using Adobe Spark Video as we can have pictures and talk about it. You'd have a picture of a deflated balloon. You're knowledge begins like a deflated balloon, as you learn it becomes bigger. Basically the balloon represents the brain.'

References and resources

Books and articles
Related to the introduction

Black, P. and Wiliam, D. (1998) 'Assessment and classroom learning', *Assessment in Education: Principles, Policy and Practice*, 5(1), pp. 7–73.

Boaler, J. (2015) *Mathematical Mindsets: Unleashing Students' Potential Through Creative Math.* USA: John Wiley & Sons, ISBN: 9780470894521.

Butler, R. (1988) 'Enhancing and undermining intrinsic motivation; the effects of task-involving and ego-involving evaluation on interest and performance', *British Journal of Educational Psychology*, 58, pp. 1–14.

Cameron, J. and Pierce, W.D. (1994) 'Reinforcement, reward and intrinsic motivation: a meta-analysis.' *Review of Educational Research*, Fall 1994, Vol. 64, pp. 3363–423.

Clarke, S. (2014) *Outstanding Formative Assessment: culture and practice.* London: Hodder Education, ISBN: 9781471829475.

Dweck, C.S. (2000) *Self-theories: Their Role in Motivation, Personality, and Development.* Hove: Psychology Press, ISBN: 9781841690247.

Dweck, C.S. (2011) 'You can grow your intelligence' article on mindsetworks.com

Dweck, C.S (2015) 'Mindsets revisited' article published online in *Education Week*, September 23, 2015.

Hattie, J. (2012) *Visible Learning for Teachers.* London: Routledge, ISBN: 9780415690157.

Woollett, K. and Maguire, E.A. (2012) 'Exploring anterograde associative memory in London taxi drivers', *NeuroReport,* 23, 15, pp. 885–8.

Related to the lessons

Andreae, G. (2014) *Giraffes Can't Dance.* London: Orchard Books, ISBN: 9781841215655.

Ashley, B. (2002) *Cleversticks.* London: HarperCollins Children's Books, ISBN: 9780006638551.

Beaty, A. (2013) *Rosie Revere Engineer.* London: Abrams Books for Young Readers, ISBN: 978-1419708459.

Brown, R. (2010) *Snail Trail.* London: Andersen Press, ISBN: 9781849392525.

Davidson, S. (2008) *Snails.* London: Usborne Publishing Ltd, ISBN: 9780746098752.

Deak, J.M. *Your Fantastic Elastic Brain.* USA: Little Pickle Press, ISBN: 9780982993804.

Jones, C.F. (2013) *Mistakes that Worked.* London: Doubleday Books, ISBN: 9780385320436.

Hood, S. (2014) *Rooting for You*. USA: Disney-Hyperion, ISBN: 9781423152309.

McCully, E.A. (1997) *Mirette on the High Wire*. London: Paperstar Book, ISBN: 9780698114432.

Pett, M. & Rubenstein, G. (2012) *The Girl Who Never Made Mistakes*. USA: Jabberwocky, ISBN: 9781402255441.

Raschka, C. (2013) *Everyone Can Learn to Ride a Bicycle*. London: Penguin Random House, ISBN: 9780375870071.

Reynolds, P.H. (2004) *The Dot*. London: Walker Books Ltd, ISBN: 9781844281695.

Turbo-Racing Team. (2013) Northampton: Igloo Books Ltd, ISBN: 9781781975374.

Further books for developing a growth mindset

Cole, B. (1990) *Three Cheers for Errol*. London: Mammoth, ISBN: 9780749701970.

Gordon, M. & Moses, B. (2013) *William Worrydactyl*. London: Wayland, ISBN: 9780750280235.

Maier, M. (2004) *When Lizzy Was Afraid of Trying New Things*. USA: Magination Press, ISBN: 9781591471714.

Moss, M. (1995) *Regina's Big Mistake*. USA: Houghton Mifflin Juvenile Books, ISBN: 9780395700938.

Reynolds, P.H. (2005) *Ish*. London: Walker Books Ltd, ISBN: 9781844282968.

Reynolds, P.A. & Reynolds, P.H. (2014) *Going Places*. USA: Atheneum Books, ISBN: 9781442466081.

Spinelli, E. (2007) *Someday*. London: Dial Books, ISBN: 9780803729414.

Thomas, P. (2010) *I Can Do It! A First Look at Not Giving Up*. USA: Barron's Educational Series, ISBN: 9780764145155.

Videos, web pages and apps

The following are arranged in the order in which they first appear in the book.

Videos

'Sesame Street: Big Bird Sings about Mistakes' by the cast of Sesame Street: youtube.com/watch?v=GHkymY6yKMg

Incy Wincy Spider nursery rhyme: youtube.com/watch?v=doyv0fL0YJw

Episode of *Charlie and Lola*: (2010) 'Too Many Big Words', *Charlie and Lola - The Absolutely Complete Collection* [DVD]. BBC.

Snail moving, to music (titled 'Snail with Music - Sunrise - Richard Strauss'): youtube.com/watch?v=Y9yffb7X9fk

Neurons firing in the brain (titled 'Neurons by David K. Anderson'): youtube.com/watch?v=TSwQOf4V3fE

The scene about what happens in the brain when you learn from *The Human Mind* (2003). BBC

More complex explanation of how the brain works: cassiopeiaproject.com/videos2.php

'There is no bathroom!' scene: (1990) *Kindergarten Cop* [DVD]. Universal Pictures

About three areas of the brain (titled 'Our Brain - Human Anatomy -Lesson for Kids- School Science Video'): youtube.com/watch?v=bLHutEdVEH4

About different parts of the brain in detail: youtube.com/watch?v=JuJy1THhqSY

Examples and further information about sketchnoting (titled 'Sketcho Frenzy: The Basics of Visual Note-taking'): youtube.com/watch?v=gY9KdRfNN9w

'Clever girl': youtube.com/watch?v=VAMQs1tjlM4

Neurons firing in the brain (titled 'Imaging reveals patterns in neuron firing'): youtube.com/watch?v=t3TaMU_qXMc

Dr. Jo Boaler discussing Maths and mistakes (titled 'Jo Boaler - Mindsets and Mistakes'): vimeo.com/103853269

Web pages

Activities to support *Rosie Revere Engineer*: andreabeaty.com

Information about Usain Bolt and his achievements: www.biography.com

Inventions that were mistakes: mag.amazing-kids.org

'Sketchnoting for Beginners' (on the iPad) by Sylvia Duckworth: sylviaduckworth.com/presentations

'The Iceberg Illusion' sketchnotes by Sylvia Duckworth: flickr.com/photos/sylviaduckworth

'Mistakes grow your brain' by Dr. Jo Boaler: youcubed.org/think-it-up

Apps

Fruit Machine: classtools.net

Random Student Selector: ehyde.com/No%20Hands

Aurasma by Hewlett-Packard: aurasma.com

Adobe Spark Video by Adobe Systems, Inc.: spark.adobe.com

Top Trump It – Make Your Own Top Trumps Card by Winning Moves UK Ltd is available on the iTunes App Store

Paper by FiftyThree - Sketch, Draw, Take Notes, Make Lists, Diagram and Wireframe by FiftyThree is available on the iTunes App Store

Apps for creating comic strips:

Make Beliefs Comix by Bill Zimmerman, Guarionex Press:
makebeliefscomix.com

Comic Book by 3DTOPO: 3dtopo.com/apps/comicbook

Toon Toolkit by Alan Clifton is available on the iTunes App Store

Marvel Kids 'Create your own comic' by Marvel: marvel.com/games/play/34/
create_your_own_comic

Pixton by Pixton Comics.: pixton.com

ToonDoo.com by Jambay: toondoo.com

To see the *Growth Mindset Lessons* videos (and many others) in full, book training courses and find out how to follow Shirley Clarke, go to shirleyclarke-education.org